AN INSPECTOR CALLS

Produced at the Opera House, Manchester, on March 9th, 1946, and subsequently at the New Theatre, London, on October 1st, 1946, with the following cast of characters:

(In the order of their appearance)

Arthur Birling	Julien Mitchell
Gerald Croft	Harry Andrews
Sheila Birling	Margaret Leighton
Sybil Birling	Marian Spencer
Edna	Marjorie Dunkels
Eric Birling	Alec Guinness
Inspector Goole	Ralph Richardson

The play produced by Basil Dean

The three acts, which are continuous, take place in the dining-room of the Birlings' house in Brumley, an industrial city in the North Midlands. An evening in Spring, 1912

NOTE: *This acting edition follows the original script of the play, in which only one set was used throughout. In the New Theatre production different aspects of the room were shown in each of the three acts. For the benefit of those companies whose scenic facilities will permit, Ground Plans and a Furniture Plot prepared in accordance with this scheme are given at the end of the book.*

An Inspector Calls

A Play

J. B. Priestley

Samuel French — London

New York – Sydney – Toronto – Hollywood

ISBN 0 573 01205 9

Please see page iv for further copyright information.

ACT I

The dining-room of the Birlings' house in Brumley, an industrial city in the North Midlands. An evening in Spring, 1912

It is the dining-room of a fairly large suburban house, belonging to a prosperous manufacturer; a solidly built square room, with good solid furniture of the period. There is only one door, which is up stage in the L. wall. Up stage C., set in an alcove, is a heavy sideboard with a silver tantalus, silver candlesticks, a silver champagne cooler and the various oddments of a dinner. The fireplace is in the R. wall. Below the door is a desk with a chair in front of it. On the wall below the fireplace is a telephone. Slightly up stage of C. is a solid but not too large dining-table, preferably oval, with a solid set of dining-room chairs round it. The table is laid with a white cloth and the closing stages of a dinner. Down stage of the fireplace is a leather armchair. A few imposing but tasteless pictures and large engravings decorate the walls, and there are light brackets above and below the fireplace and below the door. The former are lit, but the latter is not. The general effect is substantial and comfortable and old-fashioned, but not cosy and home-like (See the Ground Plan at the end of the play)

When the CURTAIN *rises, Edna, a neatly dressed parlourmaid is clearing the table of dessert plates and finger bowls, taking them to the sideboard. Arthur Birling is seated R. of the table, and Mrs Birling is L. Sheila Birling and Gerald Croft are seated above the table, R. and L. respectively. Eric Birling sits below the table. All five are in evening dress, the men in tails and white ties. Arthur Birling is a heavy-looking, rather portentous man in his middle fifties, with fairly easy manners but rather provincial in his speech. His wife is about fifty, a rather cold woman and her husband's social superior. Sheila is a pretty girl in her early twenties, very pleased with life and rather excited. Gerald Croft is an attractive chap about thirty, rather too manly to be a dandy but very much the easy well-bred young man-about-town. Eric is in his middle twenties, not quite at ease, half-shy, half-assertive. At the moment they have all had a good dinner, are celebrating a special occasion, and are pleased with themselves*

Birling Giving us the port, Edna?

Edna comes to Birling's L. with the decanter

That's right. (*He fills his glass and pushes it towards Sheila*) You ought to like this port Gerald. As a matter of fact, Finchley told me it's exactly the same port your father gets from him.

Sheila fills her glass and passes the port to Gerald

Gerald Then it'll be all right. The governor prides himself on being a
good judge of port. I don't pretend to know much about it. (*He fills his
glass and then passes the decanter towards Mrs Birling*)

Sheila (*gaily, possessively*) I should jolly well think not, Gerald. I'd hate
you to know all about port—like one of these purple-faced old men.

Birling Here, I'm not a purple-faced old man.

Sheila No, not yet. But then, you don't know all about port—do you?

Birling (*noticing that Mrs Birling has not taken any port*) Now then, Sybil,
you must take a little tonight. Special occasion, y'know, eh?

Gerald starts to fill Mrs Birling's glass

Sheila Yes, go on, Mummy. You must drink our health.

Edna picks up the tray, about to go

Mrs Birling (*smiling*) Very well, then. Just a little, thank you. (*She passes
the decanter to Eric. To Edna*) All right, Edna. I'll ring from the drawing-
room when we want coffee. Probably in about half-an-hour.

Edna (*going*) Yes, ma'am.

She goes out

*They now have all the glasses filled. Birling beams at them and clearly
relaxes*

Birling Well, well—this is very nice. Very nice. Good dinner too, Sybil.
Tell cook from me.

Gerald (*politely*) Absolutely first class.

Mrs Birling (*reproachfully*) Arthur, you're not supposed to say such things.

Birling Oh—come, come—I'm treating Gerald like one of the family. And
I'm sure he won't object.

Sheila (*with mock aggressiveness*) Go on, Gerald—just you object.

Gerald (*smiling*) Wouldn't dream of it. In fact, I insist upon being one of
the family now. I've been trying long enough, haven't I? (*As Sheila does
not reply; with more insistence*) Haven't I? You know I have.

Mrs Birling (*smiling*) Of course she does.

Sheila (*half seriously, half playfully*) Yes—except for all last summer,
when you never came near me, and I wondered what had happened to
you.

Gerald And I've told you—I was awfully busy at the works all that time.

Sheila (*in the same tone*) Yes, that's what *you* say.

Mrs Birling Now, Sheila, don't tease him. When you're married you'll
realize that men with important work to do sometimes have to spend
nearly all their time and energy on their business. You'll have to get
used to that, just as I had.

Sheila I don't believe I will. (*Half playful, half serious, to Gerald*) So you
be careful.

Gerald Oh—I will, I will.

Eric suddenly guffaws. His parents look at him

Sheila (*severely*) Now—what's the joke?

Eric I don't know—really. Suddenly I felt I just had to laugh.

Sheila You're squiffy.

Eric I'm not.

Mrs Birling What an expression, Sheila! Really, the things you girls pick up these days!

Eric If you think that's the best she can do—

Sheila Don't be an ass, Eric.

Mrs Birling Now stop it, you two. Arthur, what about this famous toast of yours?

Birling Yes, of course. (*He clears his throat*) Well, Gerald, I know you agreed that we should only have this quiet little family party. It's a pity Sir George and—er—Lady Croft can't be with us, but they're abroad and so it can't be helped. As I told you, they sent me a very nice cable—couldn't be nicer. I'm not sorry that we're celebrating quietly like this—

Mrs Birling Much nicer really.

Gerald I agree.

Birling So do I, but it makes speech-making more difficult—

Eric (*not too rudely*) Well, don't do any. We'll drink their health and have done with it.

Birling No we won't. It's one of the happiest nights of my life. And one day, I hope, Eric, when you've a daughter of your own, you'll understand why. Gerald, I'm going to tell you frankly without any pretences, that your engagement to Sheila means a tremendous lot to me. She'll make you happy. I'm sure you'll make her happy. You're just the kind of son-in-law I always wanted. Your father and I have been friendly rivals in business for some time now—though Crofts Limited are both older and bigger than Birling and Company—and now you've brought us together, and perhaps we may look forward to the time when Crofts and Birlings are no longer competing but are working together—for lower costs and higher prices.

Gerald Hear, hear! And I think my father would agree to that.

Mrs Birling Now, Arthur, I don't think you ought to talk business on an occasion like this.

Sheila Neither do I. All wrong.

Birling Quite so, I agree with you. I only mentioned it in passing. What I did want to say was—that Sheila's a lucky girl—and I think you're a pretty fortunate young man, too, Gerald.

Gerald I know I am—this once anyhow.

Birling raises his glass and rises. Mrs Birling rises

Birling So here's wishing the pair of you—the very best that life can bring. Gerald and Sheila!

Mrs Birling (*raising her glass, smiling*) Yes, Gerald. Yes, Sheila, darling. Our congratulations and very best wishes!

Gerald Thank you (*He rises*)

Mrs Birling signals to Eric to rise

Eric (*rising; rather noisily*) All the best! She's got a nasty temper sometimes—but she's not bad really. Good old Sheila!

They all sit

Sheila Chump! I can't drink to this, can I? When do I drink?
Gerald You can drink to me.
Sheila (*rising; quiet and serious now*) All right then. I drink to you,
Gerald.

For a moment Gerald and Sheila look at each other

Gerald (*quietly*) Thank you. And I drink to you—and hope I can make
you as happy as you deserve to be.
Sheila (*sitting; trying to be light and easy*) You be careful—or I'll start
weeping.
Gerald (*smiling*) Well, perhaps this will help to stop it. (*He produces a
ring case*)
Sheila (*excited*) Oh—Gerald—you've got it—is it the one you wanted me
to have?
Gerald (*giving the case to her*) Yes—the very one.
Sheila (*taking out the ring*) Oh—it's wonderful! (*She rises and crosses
behind Gerald to Mrs Birling*) Look—Mummy—isn't it a beauty? (*She
turns to Gerald*) Oh—darling—(*She slips the ring on and kisses Gerald
hastily, then crosses above him to Birling*)
Eric Steady the Buffs!
Sheila (*admiring the ring*) I think it's perfect. Now I really feel engaged.
Mrs Birling So you ought, darling. It's a lovely ring. Be careful with it.
Sheila Careful! (*She sits*) I'll never let it out of my sight for an instant.
Mrs Birling (*smiling*) Well, it came just at the right moment. That was
clever of you, Gerald. Now, Arthur, if you've no more to say, I think
Sheila and I had better go into the drawing room and leave you men—
(*She is about to rise*)
Birling (*rather heavily*) I just want to say this. (*Noticing that Sheila is still
admiring her ring*) Are you listening, Sheila? This concerns you too.
And after all I don't often make speeches at you—
Sheila I'm sorry, Daddy. Actually I was listening.

*She looks attentive, as they all do. Birling holds them for a moment before
continuing*

Birling I'm delighted about this engagement and I hope it won't be too
long before you're married. And I want to say this. There's a good deal of
silly talk about these days—*but*—and I speak as a hard-headed business
man, who has to take risks and know what he's about—I say, you can
ignore all this silly pessimistic talk. When you marry, you'll be marrying
at a very good time. Yes, a very good time—and soon it'll be an even
better time. Last month, just because the miners came out on strike,
there's a lot of wild talk about possible labour trouble in the near future.
Don't worry. We've passed the worst of it. We employers at last are
coming together to see that our interests—and the interests of Capital—

are properly protected. And we're in for a time of steadily increasing prosperity.

Gerald I believe you're right, sir.

Eric But what about war?

Birling Glad you mentioned it, Eric. I'm coming to that. Just because the Kaiser makes a speech or two, or a few German officers have too much to drink and begin talking nonsense, you'll hear some people say that war's inevitable. And to that I say—fiddlesticks! The Germans don't want war. Nobody wants war, except some half civilized folks in the Balkans. And why? There's too much at stake these days. Everything to lose and nothing to gain by war.

Eric Yes, I know—but still—

Birling Just let me finish, Eric. You've a lot to learn yet. And I'm talking as a hard-headed, practical man of business. And I say there isn't a chance of war. The world's developing so fast that it'll make war impossible. Look at the progress we're making. In a year or two we'll have aeroplanes that will be able to go anywhere. And look at the way the automobile's making headway—bigger and faster all the time. And then ships. Why, a friend of mine went over this new liner last week—the *Titanic*—she sails next week—forty-six thousand eight hundred tons—forty-six thousand eight hundred tons—New York in five days—and every luxury—and unsinkable, absolutely unsinkable. That's what you've you've got to keep your eye on, facts like that, progress like that—and not a few German officers talking nonsense and a few scaremongers here making a fuss about nothing. Now you three young people, just listen to this—and remember that I'm telling you now. In twenty or thirty years' time—let's say in 1940—you may be giving a little party like this—your son or daughter might be getting engaged—and I tell you, by that time you'll be living in a world that'll have forgotten all these Capital versus Labour agitations and all these silly little war scares. There'll be peace and prosperity and rapid progress everywhere—except of course in Russia, which will always be behindhand naturally.

Mrs Birling shows signs of interrupting

Yes, my dear—I know—I'm talking too much. But you youngsters just remember what I said. We can't let these Bernard Shaws and H. G. Wellses do all the talking. We hard-headed practical business men must say something sometimes. And we don't guess—we've had experience—and we *know*.

Mrs Birling (*rising*) Yes, of course, dear.

They all rise

Well—don't keep Gerald in here too long. (*She turns to the door*) Eric—I want you a minute.

Gerald crosses above Mrs Birling and opens the door

Mrs Birling goes out followed by Sheila and Eric

Gerald shuts the door

Birling (*crossing below the table to the desk*) Cigar? (*He takes one himself*)
Gerald (*crossing to his chair*) No, thanks. Can't really enjoy them. (*He takes a cigarette and lights it*)
Birling (*moving to the* L. *end of the table*) Ah, you don't know what you're missing. I like a good cigar. (*Indicating the decanter*) Help yourself. (*He lights his cigar*)

Gerald fills his glass and pushes the decanter towards Birling, and sits R. *above the table*

Thanks. (*He sits* L. *of the table. Confidentially*) By the way, there's something I'd like to mention—in strict confidence—while we're by ourselves. I have an idea that your mother—Lady Croft—while she doesn't object to my girl—feels you might have done better for yourself socially—

Gerald, rather embarrassed, begins to murmur some dissent, but Birling checks him

No, Gerald, that's all right. Don't blame her. She comes from an old county family—landed people and so forth—and so it's only natural. But what I wanted to say is—there's a fair chance that I might find my way into the next Honours List. Just a knighthood, of course.
Gerald Oh—I say—congratulations!
Birling Thanks. But it's a bit too early for that. So don't say anything. But I've had a hint or two. You see, I was Lord Mayor here two years ago when Royalty visited us. And I've always been regarded as a sound useful party man. So—well—I gather there's a very good chance of a knighthood—so long as we behave ourselves, don't get into the police court or start a scandal—eh? (*He laughs complacently*)
Gerald (*laughing*) You seem to be a nice well-behaved family—
Birling We think we are—
Gerald So if that's the only obstacle, sir. I think you might as well accept my congratulations now.
Birling No, no, I couldn't do that. And don't say anything yet.
Gerald Not even to my mother? I know she'd be delighted.
Birling Well, when she comes back, you might drop a hint to her. And you can promise her that we'll try to keep out of trouble during the next few months.

They both laugh

Eric enters. He stands just inside the door

Eric What's the joke? Started telling stories?
Birling No. Want another glass of port?
Eric (*closing the door and moving below the table*) Yes, please. (*He takes the decanter and helps himself*) Mother says we mustn't stay too long. But I don't think it matters. I left 'em talking about clothes again. You'd think a girl had never had any clothes before she gets married. Women are potty about 'em. (*He moves to the chair* R. *of the table and sits*)
Birling Yes, but you've got to remember, my boy, that clothes mean

something quite different to a woman. Not just something to wear—and not only something to make 'em look prettier—but—well, a sort of sign or token of their self-respect.

Gerald That's true.

Eric (*eagerly*) Yes, I remember—(*but he checks himself*)

Birling Well, what do you remember?

Eric (*confused*) Nothing.

Birling Nothing?

Gerald (*amused*) Sounds a bit fishy to me.

Birling (*taking it in the same manner*) Yes, you don't know what some of these boys get up to nowadays. More money to spend and time to spare than I had when I was Eric's age. They worked us hard in those days and kept us short of cash. Though even then—we broke out and had a bit of fun sometimes.

Gerald I'll bet you did.

Birling (*solemnly*) But this is the point. I don't want to lecture you two young fellows again. But what so many of you don't seem to understand now, when things are so much easier, is that a man has to make his own way—has to look after himself—and his family too, of course, when he has one—and so long as he does that he won't come to much harm. But the way some of these cranks talk and write now, you'd think everybody has to look after everybody else, as if we were all mixed up together like bees in a hive—community and all that nonsense. But take my word for it, you youngsters—and I've learnt in the good hard school of experience —that a man has to mind his own business and look after himself and his own—and—

We hear the sharp ring of the front door bell. Birling stops to listen

Eric Somebody at the front door.

Birling Edna'll answer it. Well, have another glass of port, Gerald—and then we'll join the ladies. That'll stop me giving you good advice.

Eric Yes, you've piled it on a bit tonight, Father.

Birling Special occasion. And feeling contented, for once, I wanted you to have the benefit of my experience.

Edna enters

Edna Please, sir, an inspector's called.

Birling An inspector? What kind of inspector?

Edna A police inspector. He says his name's Inspector Goole.

Birling Don't know him. Does he want to see me?

Edna Yes, sir. He says it's important.

Birling All right, Edna. Show him in here.

Edna goes out

I'm still on the Bench. (*As he rises and moves to the door and switches on the wall bracket over the desk*) It may be something about a warrant.

Gerald (*lightly*) Sure to be. Unless Eric's been up to something. (*Nodding confidentially to Birling*) And that would be awkward, wouldn't it?

Birling (*humorously*) Very. (*He moves in towards the table*)

Eric (*who is uneasy; sharply*) Here, what do you mean?

Gerald (*lightly*) Only something we were talking about when you were out. A joke really.

Eric (*still uneasy*) Well, I don't think it's very funny.

Birling (*staring at Eric; sharply*) What's the matter with *you*?

Eric (*defiantly*) Nothing. (*He helps himself to port*)

Edna enters

Edna (*announcing*) Inspector Goole.

The Inspector enters. He need not be a big man but he creates at once an impression of massiveness, solidity, and purposefulness. He is a man in his fifties, dressed in a plain darkish suit of the period. He speaks carefully, weightily, and has a disconcerting habit of looking hard at the person he addresses before actually speaking

Inspector Mr Birling?

Birling Yes. Sit down, Inspector.

Inspector Thank you, sir.

Edna takes the Inspector's hat and coat and goes out

Birling Have a glass of port—or a little whisky.

Inspector No, thank you, Mr Birling. I'm on duty. (*He turns the desk chair a little away from the desk and sits*)

Birling You're new, aren't you?

Inspector Yes, sir. Only recently transferred.

Birling I thought you must be. I was an alderman for years—and Lord Mayor two years ago—and I'm still on the Bench—so I know the Brumley police officers pretty well—and I thought I'd never seen you before. (*He sits L. of the table*)

Inspector Quite so.

Birling Well, what can I do for you? Some trouble about a warrant?

Inspector No, Mr Birling.

Birling (*after a pause, with a touch of impatience*) Well, what is it then?

Inspector I'd like some information, if you don't mind, Mr Birling. Two hours ago a young woman died in the Infirmary. She'd been taken there this afternoon because she'd swallowed a lot of strong disinfectant. Burnt her inside out, of course.

Eric (*involuntarily*) My God!

Inspector Yes, she was in great agony. They did everything they could for her at the Infirmary, but she died. Suicide of course.

Birling (*rather impatiently*) Yes, yes. Horrible business. But I don't understand why you should come here, Inspector—

Inspector (*cutting through, massively*) I've been round to the room she had, and she left a letter there and a sort of diary. Like a lot of these young women who get into various kinds of trouble, she'd used more than one name. But her original name—her real name—was Eva Smith.

Birling (*thoughtfully*) Eva Smith?

Inspector Do you remember her, Mr Birling?

Birling (*slowly*) No—I seem to remember hearing that name—Eva Smith —somewhere. But it doesn't convey anything to me. And I don't see where I come into this.

Inspector She was employed in your works at one time.

Birling Oh—that's it, is it? Well, we've several hundred young women there, y'know, and they keep changing.

Inspector (*rising*) This young woman, Eva Smith, was a bit out of the ordinary. I found a photograph of her in her lodgings. Perhaps you'd remember her from that. (*He takes a photograph about postcard size out of his pocket and moves towards Birling*)

Gerald rises and moves about the table to look over Birling's shoulder. Eric rises and moves below the table to see the photograph. The Inspector quickly moves above Birling and prevents both of them from seeing it. They are surprised and rather annoyed. Birling stares hard and with recognition at the photograph, which the Inspector then takes from him and replaces in his pocket, as he moves down L.C.

Gerald (*following the Inspector down; showing annoyance*) Any particular reason why I shouldn't see this girl's photograph, Inspector?

Inspector (*moving to the desk*) There might be.

Eric And the same applies to me, I suppose?

Inspector Yes.

Gerald I can't imagine what it could be.

Eric Neither can I. (*He sits below the table*)

Birling And I must say, I agree with them, Inspector.

Gerald breaks upstage

Inspector It's the way I like to go to work. (*He is watching Birling*) One person and one line of enquiry at a time. Otherwise, there's a muddle.

Birling notices the Inspector watching him

(*He moves towards Birling*) I think you remember Eva Smith now, don't you, Mr Birling?

Birling Yes, I do. She was one of my employees and then I discharged her.

Eric Is that why she committed suicide? When was this, Father?

Birling Just keep quiet, Eric, and don't get excited. This girl left us nearly two years ago. Let me see—it must have been in the early autumn of nineteen-ten.

Inspector Yes. End of September, nineteen-ten.

Birling That's right.

Gerald (*moving* C. *above the table*) Look here, sir. Wouldn't you rather I was out of this?

Birling I don't mind your being here, Gerald. And I'm sure you've no objection, have you, Inspector? Perhaps I ought to explain first that this is Mr Gerald Croft—the son of Sir George Croft—you know, Crofts Limited.

Inspector Mr Gerald Croft, eh?

Birling Yes. Incidentally we've been modestly celebrating his engagement to my daughter Sheila.

Inspector I see. (*He crosses behind Birling to Gerald*) Mr Croft is going to marry Miss Sheila Birling?

Gerald (*smiling*) I hope so.

Inspector (*gravely*) Then I'd prefer you to stay.

Gerald (*surprised*) Oh—all right. (*He sits* R. *above the table*)

Birling (*somewhat impatiently*) Look—there's nothing mysterious—or scandalous—about this business—at least not so far as I'm concerned. It's a perfectly straightforward case, and as it happened more than eighteen months ago—nearly two years ago—obviously it has nothing whatever to do with the wretched girl's suicide. Eh, Inspector?

Inspector (*coming down to the table* L. *of Gerald*) No, Sir. I can't agree with you there.

Birling Why not?

Inspector Because what happened to her then may have determined what happened to her afterwards, and what happened to her afterwards may have driven her to suicide. A chain of events.

Birling Oh well—put like that, there's something in what you say. Still, I can't accept any responsibility. If we were all responsible for everything that happened to everybody we'd had anything to do with it would be very awkward, wouldn't it?

Inspector Very awkward.

Birling We'd all be in an impossible position, wouldn't we?

Eric By jove, yes. And as you were saying, Dad, a man has to look after himself—

Birling (*rising and moving to the desk*) Yes, well, we needn't go into all that.

Inspector Go into what?

Birling Oh—just before you came—I'd been giving these young men a little good advice. Now—about this girl, Eva Smith. I remember her quite well now. She was a lively good-looking girl—country-bred, I fancy—and she'd been working in one of our machine shops for over a year. A good worker too. (*He sits at the desk*) In fact, the foreman there told me he was ready to promote her into what we call a leading operator —head of a small group of girls. But after they came back from their holidays that August, they were all rather restless, and they suddenly decided to ask for more money. They were averaging about twenty-two and six, which was neither more nor less than is paid generally in our industry. They wanted the rates raised so that they could average about twenty-five shillings a week. I refused, of course.

Inspector (*coming down* L. *of the table to Birling*) Why?

Birling (*surprised*) Did you say "Why"?

Inspector Yes. Why did you refuse?

Birling Well, Inspector, I don't see that it's any concern of yours how I choose to run my business. Is it now?

Inspector It might be, you know.

Birling (*rising*) I don't like that tone.

Inspector I'm sorry. But you asked me a question.

Birling (*crossing to the table*) And you asked me a question before that, a quite unnecessary question too.

Inspector It's my duty to ask questions.

Birling (*turning to face the Inspector*) Well, it's my duty to keep labour costs down, and if I'd agreed to this demand for a new rate we'd have added about twelve per cent to our labour costs. Does that satisfy you? (*He sits* L. *of the table*) So I refused. Said I couldn't consider it. We were paying the usual rates and if they didn't like those rates, they could go and work somewhere else. It's a free country, I told them.

Eric It isn't if you can't go and work somewhere else.

Inspector Quite so.

Birling (*to Eric*) Look—just you keep out of this. You hadn't even started in the works when this happened. So they went on strike. That didn't last long, of course.

Gerald Not if it was just after the holidays. They'd be all broke—if I know them.

Birling Right, Gerald. They mostly were. And so was the strike, after a week or two. Pitiful affair. Well, we let them all come back—at the old rates—except the four or five ringleaders, who'd started the trouble. I went down myself and told them to clear out. And this girl, Eva Smith, was one of them. She'd had a lot to say—far too much—so she had to go.

Gerald You couldn't have done anything else.

Eric He could. He could have kept her on instead of throwing her out. I call it tough luck.

Birling Rubbish! If you don't come down sharply on some of these people, they'd soon be asking for the earth.

Gerald I should say so!

Inspector They might. (*He crosses down stage to the fireplace*) But after all it's better to ask for the earth than to take it.

Birling (*staring at the Inspector*) What did you say your name was, Inspector?

Inspector Goole. (*He keeps his back to them*)

Birling How do you get on with our Chief Constable, Colonel Roberts?

Inspector I don't see much of him.

Birling Perhaps I ought to warn you that he's an old friend of mine, and that I see him fairly frequently. We play golf together sometimes up at the West Brumley.

Inspector (*drily*) I don't play golf.

Birling I didn't suppose you did.

Eric (*bursting out*) Well, I think it's a dam' shame.

Inspector (*turning to face them*) No, I've never wanted to.

Eric (*rising and crossing down* L.) No, I mean about this girl—Eva Smith. Why shouldn't they try for higher wages? We try for the highest possible prices. And I don't see why she should have been sacked just because she'd a bit more spirit than the others. You said yourself she was a good worker. I'd have let her stay.

Birling (*rather angrily*) Unless you brighten your ideas, you'll never be in a position to let anybody stay or to tell anybody to go. It's about time you learnt to face a few responsibilities. That's something this public-school-and-Varsity life you've had doesn't seem to teach you.

Eric (*crossing back to his chair and sitting; sulkily*) Well, we don't need to tell the Inspector all about that, do we?

Birling I don't see we need to tell the Inspector anything more. In fact, there's nothing I can tell him. I told the girl to clear out, and she went. That's the last I heard of her. Have you any ideas what happened to her after that? Get into trouble? Go on the streets?

Inspector (*rather slowly*) No, she didn't exactly go on the streets.

Sheila enters, overhearing these last words

Sheila (*gaily*) What's this about streets?

Gerald rises and crosses to the door

(*She notices the Inspector*) Oh—sorry. I didn't know. Mummy sent me in to ask you why you didn't come along to the drawing-room.

Birling We shall be along in a minute now. Just finishing.

Inspector I'm afraid not.

Birling (*abruptly*) There's nothing else, y'know. I've just told you that.

Sheila What's all this about?

Birling (*rising and moving to Sheila*) Nothing to do with you, Sheila. Run along.

Inspector No, wait a minute, Miss Birling.

Birling (*angrily*) Look here, Inspector, I consider this uncalled for and officious. I've half a mind to report you. I've told you all I know—and it doesn't seem to me very important—and now there isn't the slightest reason why my daughter should be dragged into this unpleasant business.

Sheila (*crossing Birling to* L. *of the table*) What business? What's happening?

Inspector (*impressively*) I'm a police inspector, Miss Birling. This afternoon a young woman drank some disinfectant, and died, after several hours of agony, tonight in the Infirmary.

Sheila Oh—how horrible! Was it an accident?

Inspector No. She wanted to end her life. She felt she couldn't go on any longer.

Birling (*coming down to the desk and sitting*) Well, don't tell me that's because I discharged her from my employment nearly two years ago.

Eric That might have started it.

Sheila Did you, Dad?

Birling Yes.

Sheila sits L. *of the table*

The girl had been causing trouble in the works. I was quite justified.

Gerald Yes, I think you were. (*He moves above the table*) I know we'd have done the same thing. Don't look like that, Sheila.

Sheila (*rather distressed*) Sorry! It's just that I can't help thinking about this girl—destroying herself so horribly—and I've been so happy tonight. (*To the Inspector*) Oh I wish you hadn't told me. What was she like? Quite young?

Inspector Yes. (*He crosses slowly below the table towards* L.) Twenty-four.

Sheila Pretty.

Inspector (*moving up* L. *of Sheila*) She wasn't pretty when I saw her today but she had been pretty—very pretty. (*He continues above the table*)

Birling That's enough of that.

Gerald (*moving away* R. *of the table*) And I don't really see that this enquiry gets you anywhere, Inspector. It's what happened to her since she left Mr Birling's works that is important.

Birling Obviously. I suggested that some time ago.

Gerald And we can't help you there because we don't know.

He sits R. *of the table*

Inspector (*slowly*) Are you sure you don't know? (*He looks at Gerald, then at Eric, then at Sheila. Then he comes down to the table between the two chairs above it*)

Birling (*rising*) And are you suggesting now that one of them knows something about this girl?

Inspector Yes.

Birling You didn't come here just to see me then?

Inspector No.

The other four exchange bewildered and perturbed glances. Birling rises

Birling (*moving above Sheila's chair; with a marked change of tone*) Well, of course, if I'd known that earlier, I wouldn't have called you officious and talked about reporting you. You understand that, don't you, Inspector. I thought that—for some reason best known to yourself—you were making the most of this tiny bit of information I could give you. I'm sorry. This makes a difference. You're sure of your facts?

Inspector Some of them—yes.

Birling I can't think they can be of any great consequence.

Inspector The girl's dead, though.

Sheila What do you mean by saying that? You talk as if we were responsible—

Birling (*cutting in*) Just a minute, Sheila. Now, Inspector, perhaps you and I had better go and talk this over quietly in a corner—

Sheila (*cutting in*) Why should you? He's finished with you. He says it's one of us now.

Birling Yes, and I'm trying to settle it sensibly for you.

Gerald Well, there's nothing to settle as far as I'm concerned. I've never known an Eva Smith.

Eric Neither have I.

Sheila Was that her name? Eva Smith?

Gerald Yes.

Sheila Never heard it before.

Gerald So where are you now, Inspector?

Inspector Where I was before, Mr Croft. I told you—that like a lot of these young women, she'd used more than one name. She was still Eva Smith when Mr Birling sacked her—for wanting twenty-five shillings a week instead of twenty-two and six. But after that she stopped being Eva Smith. Perhaps she'd had enough of it.

Eric I can't blame her.

Sheila (*to Birling*) I think it was a mean thing to do. Perhaps that spoilt everything for her.

Birling Rubbish! (*He comes down to the desk. To the Inspector*) Do you know what happened to this girl after she left my works? (*He sits*)

Inspector Yes. She was out of work for the next two months. Both her parents were dead so that she'd no home to go back to. And she hadn't been able to save much out of what Birling and Company had paid her. So that after two months, with no work, no money coming in, and living in lodgings, with no relatives to help her, few friends, lonely, half-starved, she was feeling desperate.

Sheila (*warmly*) I should think so. It's a rotten shame.

Inspector There are a lot of young women living that sort of existence in every city and big town in this country, Miss Birling. If there weren't, the factories and warehouses wouldn't know where to look for cheap labour. Ask your father.

Sheila But these girls aren't cheap labour—they're *people*.

Inspector (*moving round the table to Birling; drily*) I'd had that notion myself from time to time. In fact, I've thought that it would do us all a bit of good if sometimes we tried to put ourselves in the place of these young women counting their pennies in their dingy little back bedrooms.

Sheila Yes, I expect it would. But what happened to her then?

Inspector She had what seemed to her a wonderful stroke of luck. She was taken on in a shop—and a good shop too—Milwards.

Sheila Milwards! We go there—in fact, I was there this afternoon— (*archly, to Gerald*)—for *your* benefit.

Gerald (*smiling*) Good!

Inspector There was a good deal of influenza about at that time and Milwards suddenly found themselves short-handed. So that gave her her chance. And from what I can gather, she liked working there. It was a nice change from a factory. She enjoyed being among pretty clothes, I've no doubt. And now she felt she was making a good fresh start. You can imagine how she felt.

Sheila Yes, of course.

Birling And then she got herself into trouble there, I suppose.

Inspector (*moving to* L. *of Sheila*) After about a couple of months, just when she felt she was settling down nicely, they told her she'd have to go.

Birling Not doing her work properly?

Inspector There was nothing wrong with the way she was doing her work. They admitted that.

Birling There must have been something wrong.

Inspector All she knew was—that a customer complained about her—and so she had to go.

Sheila (*staring at him; agitatedly*) When was this?

Inspector (*impressively*) At the end of January—last year.

Sheila What—what did this girl look like?

Inspector If you'll come over here, I'll show you. (*He moves to the door.*)

Sheila rises and moves to the Inspector. Gerald rises and moves c. above the table. The Inspector produces the photograph.

Sheila looks at it closely, recognizes it with a little cry, gives a half-startled sob, and then opens the door and runs out

The Inspector puts the photograph back into his pocket and stares speculatively after her. The other three stare in amazement for a moment

Birling (*rising*) What's the matter with her?

Gerald moves towards the Inspector

Eric (*rising and moving round the table to* L.; *to the Inspector*) She recognized her from the photograph, didn't she?

Inspector Yes.

Birling (*angrily*) Why the devil do you want to go upsetting the child like that?

Inspector I did nothing. She's upsetting herself. (*He comes down between Birling and Eric and moves* C.)

Birling Well—why—why?

Inspector (*crossing down* R.) I don't know—yet. That's something I have to find out.

Birling (*still angrily*) Well—if you don't mind—I'll find out first.

Gerald (*moving to the door; to Birling*) Shall I go to her?

Birling (*moving to the door*) No, leave this to me. I must also have a word with my wife—tell her what's happening. (*He comes down* L.C. *towards the Inspector*) We were having a nice little family celebration tonight. And a nasty mess you've made of it now, haven't you?

Gerald moves above the table

Inspector (*steadily*) That's more or less what I was thinking earlier tonight, when I was in the Infirmary looking at what was left of Eva Smith. A nice little promising life there, I thought, and a nasty mess somebody's made of it. (*He crosses to the desk*)

Birling looks as if he is about to make some retort, then thinks better of it and goes out, closing the door sharply behind him

Gerald and Eric exchange uneasy glances. Eric sits below the table

Gerald (*coming down* L. *of the table to the Inspector*) I'd like to have a look at that photograph now, Inspector.

Inspector All in good time.

Gerald I don't see why—

Inspector (*turning to him; cutting in massively*) You heard what I said before, Mr Croft. One line of enquiry at a time. Otherwise we'll all be talking at once and won't know where we are.

Gerald moves up to the sideboard

Eric (*rising and moving* L. *of the table; suddenly bursting out*) Look here, I've had enough of this.

Inspector (*drily*) I dare say.

Eric (*moving to the Inspector; uneasily*) I'm sorry—but you see—we were having a little party—and I've had a few drinks, including rather a lot of champagne—and I've got a headache—and as I'm only in the way here—I think I'd better turn in. (*He moves to the door*)

Inspector And I think you'd better stay here.

Eric Why should I?

Inspector It might be less trouble. If you turn in, you might have to turn out again soon.

Gerald Getting a bit heavy-handed, aren't you, Inspector?

Inspector Possibly. But if you're easy with me, I'm easy with you.

Gerald After all, y'know, we're respectable citizens and not criminals.

Inspector Sometimes there isn't as much difference as you think. Often, if it was left to me, I wouldn't know where to draw the line.

Gerald Fortunately, it isn't left to you, is it?

Inspector No, it isn't. But some things are left to me. Enquiries of this sort, for instance.

Eric crosses below the table to C.

Sheila enters. She looks as if she has been crying

Well, Miss Birling? •

Sheila (*closing the door*) You knew it was me all the time, didn't you?

Inspector I had an idea it might be—from something the girl herself wrote.

Sheila I've told my father—he didn't seem to think it amounted to much—but I felt rotten about it at the time and now I feel a lot worse. (*She moves to the* L. *end of the table*) Did it make much difference to her?

Inspector Yes, I'm afraid it did. It was the last really steady job she had. When she lost it—for no reason that she could discover—she decided she might as well try another kind of life. (*He moves to Sheila*)

Sheila (*miserably*) So I'm really responsible?

Inspector No, not entirely. A good deal happened to her after that. But you're partly to blame. Just as your father is.

Sheila sits L. *of the table*

Eric But what did Sheila do?

Sheila (*distressed*) I went to the manager at Milwards and I told him that if they didn't get rid of that girl, I'd never go near the place again and I'd persuade mother to close our account with them.

Inspector And why did you do that?

Sheila Because I was in a furious temper.

Inspector And what had this girl done to make you lose your temper?

Sheila When I was looking at myself in the mirror I caught sight of her smiling at the assistant, and I was furious with her. I'd been in a bad temper anyhow.

Inspector And was it the girl's fault?

Sheila No, not really. It was my own fault. (*Suddenly to Gerald*) All right, Gerald, you needn't look at me like that. At least, I'm trying to tell the truth. I expect you've done things you're ashamed of too.

Gerald (*surprised*) Well, I never said I hadn't. (*He comes to the table*) I don't see why—

Inspector (*cutting in*) Never mind about that. You can settle that between you afterwards.

Gerald sits L. *above the table*

(*To Sheila*) What happened?

Sheila I'd gone in to try something on. It was an idea of my own—mother had been against it, and so had the assistant—but I insisted. As soon as I tried it on, I knew they'd been right. It just didn't suit me at all. I looked silly in the thing. Well, this girl had brought the dress up from the workroom, and when the assistant—Miss Francis—had asked her something about it, this girl, to show us what she meant, had held the dress up, as if she was wearing it. And it just suited her. She was the right type for it, just as I was the wrong type. She was a very pretty girl too—with soft fine hair and big grey eyes—and that didn't make it any better. Well, when I tried the thing on and looked at myself and knew that it was all wrong, I caught sight of this girl smiling at Miss Francis— as if to say, "Doesn't she look awful"—and I was absolutely furious. I was very rude to both of them, and then I went to the manager and told him that this girl had been very impertinent—and—(*She almost breaks down, but just controls herself*) How could I know what would happen afterwards? If she'd been some miserable plain little creature, I don't suppose I'd have done it. But she was very pretty and looked as if she could take care of herself. I couldn't be sorry for her.

Inspector In fact, in a kind of way, you might be said to have been jealous of her.

Sheila Yes, I suppose so.

Inspector And so you used the power you had, as the daughter of a good customer and of a man well-known in the town, to punish the girl just because she made you feel like that.

Sheila Yes, but it didn't seem to be anything very terrible at the time. Don't you understand? And if I could help her now, I would—

Inspector (*moving up stage to the sideboard; harshly*) Yes, but you can't. It's too late. She's dead.

Eric (*crossing to the fireplace*) My God, it's a bit thick, when you come to think of it—(*He sits in the armchair*)

Sheila (*stormily*) Oh shut up, Eric. I know, I know. It's the only time I've ever done anything like that, and I'll never do it again to anybody. I've noticed them giving me a sort of look sometimes at Milwards—I noticed it even this afternoon—and I suppose some of them remember. I feel now I can never go there again. Oh—why had this to happen?

Inspector (*coming down* R. *of the table; sternly*) That's what I asked myself tonight when I was looking at that dead girl. And then I said to

myself, "Well, we'll try to understand why it had to happen." And that's
why I'm here, and why I'm not going until I know *all* that happened.
(*He sits* R. *of the table*) Eva Smith lost her job with Birling and Company
because the strike failed and they were determined not to have another
one. At last she found another job—under what name I don't know—
in a big shop, and had to leave there because you were annoyed with
yourself and passed the annoyance on to her. Now she had to try something else. So first she changed her name to Daisy Renton—

Gerald (*startled*) What?

Inspector (*steadily*) I said she changed her name to Daisy Renton.

*Gerald rises, moves up to the sideboard and pours himself out a whisky
which he drinks*

Inspector (*rising and crossing below the table to* C.) Where is your father,
Miss Birling?

Sheila He went into the drawing-room, to tell my mother what was
happening here. Eric, take the Inspector along to the drawing-room.

Eric rises, crosses to the door and opens it

*The Inspector crosses to the door, looks from Sheila to Gerald, then goes
out with Eric*

Gerald comes down R. *of the table*

Well, Gerald?

Gerald (*trying to smile*) Well, what, Sheila?

Sheila How did you come to know this girl—Eva Smith?

Gerald I didn't.

Sheila Daisy Renton then—it's the same thing.

Gerald Why should I have known her?

Sheila Oh don't be stupid. We haven't much time. You gave yourself
away as soon as he mentioned her other name.

Gerald (*moving in to* R. *of the table*) All right. I knew her. Let's leave it at
that.

Sheila We can't leave it at that.

Gerald Now listen, darling—

Sheila No, that's no use. You not only knew her but you knew her very
well. Otherwise, you wouldn't look so guilty about it. When did you
first get to know her?

Gerald does not reply. He sits R. *of the table*

Was it after she left Milwards? When she changed her name, as he said,
and began to lead a different life? Were you seeing her last Spring and
Summer, during that time when you hardly came near me and said you
were so busy? Were you?

Gerald does not reply, but looks at her

Yes, of course you were. (*She rises and comes slowly down* L.)

Gerald I'm sorry, Sheila. But it was all over and done with last Summer.

I hadn't set eyes on the girl for at least six months. I don't come into this suicide business.

Sheila I thought I didn't half-an-hour ago.

Gerald You don't. Neither of us does. So—for God's sake—don't say anything to the Inspector.

Sheila (*turning to him*) About you and this girl?

Gerald Yes. We can keep it from him.

Sheila laughs rather hysterically. She crosses to the chair below the table and kneels on it

Sheila Why—you fool—*he knows*. Of course he knows. And I hate to think how much he knows that we don't know yet. You'll see. You'll see. (*She looks at him almost in triumph*)

Gerald looks crushed

   The door slowly opens and the Inspector appears, looking steadily and searching at them

Gerald rises

                              The CURTAIN *falls*

ACT II

The same. The action is continuous

When the CURTAIN *rises Gerald has just risen; the Inspector is still at the door looking at Sheila and Gerald. Then he comes forward a step, leaving the door open behind him*

Inspector (*to Gerald*) Well?

Sheila (*crossing to the fireplace; with an hysterical laugh, to Gerald*) You see? What did I tell you?

Inspector What did you tell him? (*He closes the door*)

Gerald (*moving below the table; with an effort*) Inspector, I think Miss Birling ought to be excused any more of this questioning. She's had a exciting and tiring day—we were celebrating our engagement, you know—and now she's obviously had about as much as she can stand. You heard her.

Sheila He means that I'm getting hysterical now.

Inspector And are you?

Sheila Probably.

Inspector Well, I don't want to keep you here. (*He moves down* L.) I've no more questions to ask you.

Sheila No, but you haven't finished asking questions—have you?

Inspector No.

Sheila (*to Gerald*) You see? (*To the Inspector*) Then I'm staying.

Gerald Why should you? It's bound to be unpleasant and disturbing.

Inspector (*turning to Gerald*) And you think young women ought to be protected against unpleasant and disturbing things?

Gerald If possible—yes.

Inspector (*moving up* L. *of the table to the sideboard*) Well, we know one young woman who wasn't, don't we?

Gerald I suppose I asked for that.

Sheila Be careful you don't ask for any more, Gerald.

Gerald I only meant to say to you—Why stay when you'll hate it?

Sheila It can't be any worse for me than it has been. And it might be better.

Gerald (*bitterly*) I see.

Sheila What do you see?

Gerald You've been through it—and now you want to see somebody else put through it.

Sheila (*bitterly*) So that's what you think I'm really like. I'm glad I realized it in time, Gerald.

Gerald (*moving away down* L.) No, no, I didn't mean—

Sheila (*crossing to Gerald; cutting in*) Yes, you did. And if you'd really loved me, you couldn't have said that. You listened to that nice story about me. I got that girl sacked from Milwards. And now you've made up your mind I must obviously be a selfish vindictive creature.

Gerald I neither said that nor even suggested it.

Sheila Then why say I want to see somebody else put through it? That's not what I meant at all. (*She sits below the table*)

Gerald All right then, I'm sorry.

Sheila Yes, but you don't believe me. And this is just the wrong time not to believe me.

Inspector (*coming down* L. *of the table; massively taking charge*) Allow me, Miss Birling. (*To Gerald*) I can tell you why Miss Birling wants to stay on and why she says it might be better for her if she did. A girl died tonight. A pretty, lively sort of girl, who never did anybody any harm. But she died in misery and agony—hating life—

Sheila (*distressed*) Don't, please—I know, I know—and I can't stop thinking about it—

Inspector (*ignoring this*) Now, Miss Birling has just been made to understand what she did to this girl. She feels responsible. And if she leaves us now, and doesn't hear any more, then she'll feel she's entirely to blame, she'll be alone with her responsibility, the rest of tonight, all tomorrow, all the next night—

Sheila (*eagerly*) Yes, that's it. And I know I'm to blame—and I'm desperately sorry—but I can't believe—I won't believe—it's simply my fault that in the end she—she committed suicide. That would be too horrible—

Inspector (*sternly to them both*) You see, we have to share something. If there's nothing else, we'll have to share our guilt. (*He crosses to the fireplace*)

Gerald moves to Sheila

Sheila (*rising; staring at the Inspector*) Yes. That's true. You know. (*She goes closer to him, wonderingly*) I don't understand about you.

Inspector (*calmly*) There's no reason why you should.

Sheila I don't know much about police inspectors—but the ones I have met weren't a bit like you.

Inspector And, in a way, it's a pity, isn't it?

Sheila (*wonderingly*) Yes, that's the strange part of it. (*She looks at him curiously, and talks almost to herself*) I was just going to say something like that. They weren't but perhaps they ought to have been. As if—suddenly—there came a real one—at last. And that's absurd, isn't it?

Inspector (*calmly*) Is it? (*He regards her calmly*)

Sheila stares at him wonderingly and dubiously

Mrs Birling enters, briskly and self-confidently, quite out of key with the little scene which has just passed

Shelia feels this at once

Mrs Birling (*closing the door; smiling and social*) Good evening, Inspector.

Gerald moves up L. *of the table to the sideboard*

Inspector Good evening, Madam.

Mrs Birling (*in the same easy tone*) I'm Mrs Birling, y'know. (*She comes down* L.C.) My husband has just explained why you're here and while we'll be glad to tell you anything you want to know, I don't think we can help you much.

Sheila (*crossing to Mrs Birling*) No, Mother—please!

Mrs Birling (*affecting great surprise*) What's the matter, Sheila?

Sheila (*hesitantly*) I know it sounds silly—

Mrs Birling What does?

Sheila You see, I feel you're beginning all wrong. And I'm afraid you'll say something or do something that you'll be sorry for afterwards.

Mrs Birling I don't know what you're talking about, Sheila.

Sheila We all started like that—so confident, so pleased with ourselves until he began asking us questions.

Mrs Birling looks from Sheila to the Inspector and crosses to him

Mrs Birling You seem to have made a great impression on this child, Inspector.

Inspector (*coolly*) We often do on the young ones. They're more impressionable.

He and Mrs Birling look at each other for a moment. Then Mrs Birling turns to Sheila again

Mrs Birling You're looking tired, dear. (*She moves* C. *below the table*) I think you ought to go to bed—and forget about this absurd business. You'll feel better in the morning.

Sheila Mother, I couldn't possibly go. Nothing could be worse for me. We've settled all that. I'm staying here until I know why that girl killed herself.

Mrs Birling (*sitting below the table*) Nothing but morbid curiosity.

Sheila No it isn't.

Mrs Birling Please don't contradict me like that. And in any case I don't suppose for a moment that we can understand why the girl committed suicide. Girls of that class—

Sheila (*cutting in; urgently*) Mother, don't—please don't. For your own sake, as well as ours, you mustn't—

Mrs Birling (*annoyed*) Mustn't—what? Really, Sheila!

Sheila (*sitting* L. *of the table; slowly, carefully now*) You mustn't try to build up a kind of wall between us and that girl. If you do, then the Inspector will just break it down. And it'll be all the worse when he does.

Mrs Birling I don't understand you. (*To the Inspector*) Do you?

Inspector Yes. And she's right.

Mrs Birling (*haughtily*) I beg your pardon!

Inspector (*crossing to Mrs Birling; very plainly*) I said, Yes—I do understand her. And she's right.

Mrs Birling That—I consider—is a trifle impertinent, Inspector.

Sheila gives a short hysterical laugh

Now, what is it, Sheila?

Gerald comes down to the back of Sheila's chair

Sheila I don't know. Perhaps it's because *impertinent* is such a silly word. But, Mother, do stop before it's too late.

Mrs Birling If you mean that the Inspector will take offence—

Inspector (*cutting in; calmly*) No, no. I never take offence.

Mrs Birling I'm glad to hear it. Though I must add that it seems to me that we have more reason for taking offence.

Inspector Let's leave *offence* out of it, shall we?

Gerald I think we'd better.

Sheila So do I.

Mrs Birling (*rebuking them*) *I'm* talking to the Inspector now, if you don't mind. (*To the Inspector, rather grandly*) I realize that you may have to conduct some sort of enquiry, but I must say that so far you seem to be conducting it in a rather peculiar and offensive manner. You know of course that my husband was Lord Mayor only two years ago and that he's still a magistrate—

Gerald (*cutting in; rather impatiently*) Mrs Birling, the Inspector knows all that. And I don't think it's a very good idea to remind him—

Sheila (*cutting in*) It's crazy. Stop it, please, Mother.

Inspector They're right, y'know.

Mrs Birling (*trying to crush him*) Indeed!

Inspector (*imperturbably*) Yes. (*He crosses down* L.) Now what about Mr Birling?

Mrs Birling He's coming back in a moment. He's just talking to my son, Eric, who seems to be in an excitable silly mood.

Inspector What's the matter with him?

Mrs Birling Eric? Oh—I'm afraid he may have had rather too much to drink tonight. We were having a little celebration here—

Inspector (*cutting in*) Isn't he used to drinking?

Mrs Birling No, of course not. He's only a boy.

Inspector No, he's a young man. And some young men drink far too much.

Sheila And Eric's one of them.

Mrs Birling (*very sharply*) Sheila!

Sheila (*rising and crossing below the table to the fireplace; urgently*) I don't want to get poor Eric into trouble. He's probably in enough trouble already. But we really must stop these silly pretences. This isn't the time to pretend that Eric isn't used to drink. He's been steadily drinking too much for the last two years.

Mrs Birling (*staggered*) It isn't true. You know him, Gerald—and you're a man—you must know it isn't true.

Gerald hesitates

Inspector Well, Mr Croft?

Gerald (*apologetically to Mrs Birling*) I'm afraid it is, y'know. Actually I've never seen much of him outside this house—but—well, I have gathered that he does drink pretty hard.

Mrs Birling (*rising and crossing to Sheila; bitterly*) And this is the time you choose to tell me.

Sheila Yes, of course it is. That's what I meant when I talked about building up a wall that's sure to be knocked flat. It makes it all the harder to bear.

Mrs Birling But it's you—and not the Inspector here—who's doing it—

Sheila Yes, but don't you see? *He hasn't started on you yet.*

Mrs Birling (*after a pause; recovering herself*) If necessary I shall be glad to answer any questions the Inspector wishes to ask me. Though naturally I don't know anything about this girl.

Inspector (*gravely*) We'll see, Mrs Birling.

Birling enters. He closes the door behind him

Birling (*rather hot, bothered*) I've been trying to persuade Eric to go to bed, but he won't. (*To the Inspector*) Now he says you told him to stay up. Did you?

Inspector Yes, I did.

Birling Why?

Inspector Because I shall want to talk to him, Mr Birling.

Birling (*crossing above the table to the fireplace*) I don't see why you should, but if you must, then I suggest you do it now. Have him in and get it over, then let the lad go.

Inspector No, I can't do that yet. I'm sorry, but he'll have to wait.

Birling Now look here, Inspector—

Inspector (*moving* C. *below the table; cutting in; with authority*) He must wait his turn.

Sheila (*sitting in armchair; to Mrs Birling*) You see?

Mrs Birling No, I don't. And please be quiet, Sheila.

Birling (*angrily*) Inspector. I've told you before, I don't like your tone nor the way you're handling this enquiry. And I don't propose to give you much more rope.

Inspector You needn't give me any rope.

Sheila (*rather wildly, with a laugh*) No, he's giving us rope—so that we'll hang ourselves.

Birling (*to Mrs Birling*) What's the matter with that child?

Mrs Birling Over-excited. And she refuses to go. (*With sudden anger; to the Inspector*) Well, come along—what is it you want to know?

Inspector (*moving slowly down* L.; *coolly*) At the end of January, last year, this girl Eva Smith had to leave Milwards, because Miss Birling compelled them to discharge her, and then she stopped being Eva Smith, looking for a job and became Daisy Renton, with other ideas. (*Turning on Gerald, sharply*) Mr Croft, when did you first get to know her?

There is an exclamation of surprise from Birling and Mrs Birling

Gerald Where did you get the idea that I did know her?

Sheila It's no use, Gerald. You're wasting time.

Inspector As soon as I mentioned the name Daisy Renton, it was obvious you'd known her. You gave yourself away at once.

Sheila (*rising and moving to the chair below the table; bitterly*) Of course he did.

Inspector And anyhow I knew already. When and where did you first meet her?

Gerald All right, if you must have it. (*He sits* L. *of the table*) I met her first, sometime in March last year, in the stalls bar at the Palace. I mean the Palace music hall here in Brumley—

Sheila (*moving* R. *round the table and above it*) Well, we didn't think you meant Buckingham Palace.

Gerald (*to Sheila*) Thanks. You're going to be a great help, I can see. You've said your piece, and you're obviously going to hate this, so why on earth don't you leave us to it?

Sheila Nothing would induce me. I want to understand exactly what happens when a man says he's so busy at the works that he can hardly ever find time to come and see the girl he's supposed to be in love with. I wouldn't miss it for—

Inspector (*with authority*) Be quiet, please.

Sheila moves up to the sideboard

(*He crosses to the chair below the table and sits*) Yes, Mr Croft—in the stalls bar at the Palace Variety Theatre . . .

Gerald I happened to look in, one night, after a rather long dull day, and as the show wasn't very bright, I went down into the bar for a drink. It's a favourite haunt of women of the town—

Mrs Birling Women of the town?

Inspector Prostitutes.

Mrs Birling Yes—but here—in Brumley—

Inspector One of the worst cities in the country for prostitution.

Birling Quite true. But I see no point in mentioning the subject—especially —(*indicating Sheila*)

Mrs Birling It would be much better if Sheila didn't listen to this story at all.

Sheila But you're forgetting I'm supposed to be engaged to the hero of it. Go on, Gerald. (*She comes down to the back of Gerald's chair*) You went down into the bar, which is a favourite haunt of women of the town.

Gerald I'm glad I amuse you—

Inspector (*sharply*) Come along, Mr Croft. What happened?

Gerald I didn't propose to stay long down there. I hate those hard-eyed, dough-faced women. But then I noticed a girl who looked quite different. She was very pretty—soft brown hair and big grey eyes—(*he breaks off*) My God!

Inspector What's the matter.

Gerald (*distressed*) Sorry—I—well, I've suddenly realized—taken it in properly—that she's dead—

Inspector (*harshly*) Yes, she's dead

Sheila And probably between us we killed her.

Mrs Birling (*sitting in the armchair; sharply*) Sheila, don't talk nonsense.

Inspector (*to Gerald*) Go on.

Gerald This girl was young and pretty and—well—quite out of place down there. And obviously she wasn't enjoying herself. Old Joe Meggarty, half-drunk and goggle-eyed, had wedged her into a corner with that obscene fat carcase of his—

Mrs Birling (*cutting in*) There's no need to be disgusting. And surely you don't mean Alderman Meggarty?

Gerald Of course I do. He's a notorious womaniser as well as being one of the worst sots and rogues in Brumley.

Inspector Quite right.

Mrs Birling (*staggered*) Well, really! Alderman Meggarty! I must say, we *are* learning something tonight.

Sheila (*coolly*) Of course we are. But everybody knows about that horrible old Meggarty. A girl I know had to see him at the Town Hall one afternoon and she only escaped with a torn blouse—

Birling (*shocked; sharply*) Sheila!

Inspector (*to Gerald*) Go on.

Gerald The girl saw me looking at her and then gave me a glance that was nothing less than a cry for help. So I went across and told Joe Meggarty some nonsense—that the manager had a message for him or something like that—got him out of the way—and then told the girl that if she didn't want any more of that sort of thing, she'd better let me take her our of there. She agreed at once. (*He rises and moves down* L.)

Inspector Where did you go?

Gerald We went along to the County Hotel, which I knew would be quiet at that time of night, and we had a drink or two and talked.

Inspector Did she drink much at that time?

Gerald No. She only had a port and lemonade—or some such concoction. (*He turns to the Inspector*) All she wanted was to talk—a little friendliness—and I gathered that Joe Meggarty's advances had left her rather shaken—as well they might—

Inspector She talked about herself?

Gerald Yes. I asked her questions about herself. She told me her name was Daisy Renton, that she'd lost both parents, and that she came originally from somewhere outside Brumley. She also told me she'd had a job in one of the works here and had had to leave after a strike. She said something about the shop too but wouldn't say which it was, and she was deliberately vague about what happened. I couldn't get any exact details from her about her past life. (*He moves in to* L. *of the table*) She wanted to talk about herself—just because she felt I was interested and friendly—but at the same time she wanted to be Daisy Renton—and not Eva Smith. In fact, I heard that name for the first time tonight. What she did let slip—though she didn't mean to—was that she was desperately hard up and at that moment was actually hungry. I made the people at the "County" find some food for her.

Inspector And then you decided to keep her—as your mistress?

Mrs Birling What?

Sheila (*coming down* L.) Of course, Mother. It was obvious from the start. Go on, Gerald. Don't mind Mother.

Birling turns the chair from R. *of the table to the fire and sits*

Gerald (*steadily*) I discovered, not that night but two nights later, when we met again—not accidentally this time of course—that in fact she hadn't a penny and was going to be turned out of the miserable back-room she had. It happened that a friend of mine had gone off to Canada for six months and had let me have the key of a flat of his. So I insisted on Daisy moving into it and made her take some money to keep her going there. (*He sits* L. *of the table. Carefully, to the Inspector*) I want you to understand that I didn't install her there so that I could make love to her. That came afterwards. I made her go there because I was sorry for her, and didn't like the idea of her going back to the Palace bar. I didn't ask for anything in return.

Inspector I see. (*He rises and moves* R. *round the table up to the sideboard*)

Sheila (*to Gerald*) Yes, but why are you saying that to him? You ought to be saying it to me.

Gerald I suppose I ought, really. I'm sorry, Sheila. Somehow I—(*He hesitates*)

Sheila (*cutting in*) I know. Somehow he makes you.

Inspector (*to Gerald*) But she became your mistress?

Gerald Yes. I suppose it was inevitable.

Sheila moves to the desk

She was young and pretty and warm-hearted—and intensely grateful. I became at once the most important person in her life—you understand?

Inspector Yes. She was a woman. She was lonely. You'd been friendly and looked after her. And women want somebody to love. It's their weakness.

Sheila That's a nice thing to say.

Inspector The world being what it is—a battlefield rather than a home—this desire of women to love is a weakness. In another kind of world, it might be a source of strength. But not in the world we've made. (*To Gerald*) Were you in love with her?

Sheila Just what I was going to ask.

Birling (*rising; angrily*) I really must protest—

Inspector (*turning on him sharply*) Why should you do any protesting? It was you who turned the girl out in the first place.

Birling (*rather taken aback*) Well, I only did what any employer might have done. And what I was going to say was that I protest against the way in which my daughter, a young unmarried girl, is being dragged into this—

Inspector (*sharply*) Your daughter isn't living on the moon. She's here in Brumley too. (*He comes down to the back of Gerald's chair*)

Sheila Yes, and it was I who had the girl turned out of her job at Milwards.

And I'm supposed to be engaged to Gerald. And I'm not a child, don't forget. I've a right to know. (*She moves to Gerald*) *Were* you in love with her, Gerald?

Gerald (*hesitantly*) It's hard to say. I didn't feel about her as she felt about me.

Sheila (*breaking away to* C. *below the table; with sharp sarcasm*) Of course not. You were the wonderful Fairy Prince. You must have adored it, Gerald.

Gerald All right—I did for a time. Almost any man would have done.

Sheila (*turning to Gerald*) That's probably about the best thing you've said tonight. At least it's honest. Did you go and see her every night? (*She sits below the table*)

Gerald No. I wasn't telling you a complete lie when I said I'd been very busy at the works all that time. We were very busy. But of course I did see a good deal of her.

Mrs Birling (*rising*) I don't think we want any further details of this disgusting affair—

The Inspector moves slowly down L.

Sheila (*cutting in*) I do. And anyhow we haven't had any details yet.

Gerald (*rising*) And you're not going to have any. (*To Mrs Birling*) You know, it wasn't disgusting.

Mrs Birling It was disgusting to me.

Sheila Yes, but after all, you didn't come into this, did you, Mother?

Gerald (*coming down to the Inspector*) Is there anything else you want to know—that you ought to know?

Inspector Yes. When did this affair end?

Gerald In the first week of September. I had to go away for several weeks then—on business—and by that time Daisy knew it was coming to an end. So I broke it off definitely before I went.

Inspector How did she take it?

Gerald Better than I'd hoped. She was—very gallant—about it.

Sheila (*with irony*) That was nice for you.

Gerald No it wasn't (*He waits a moment; then in a low troubled tone*) She told me she'd been happier than she'd ever been before—but that she knew it couldn't last—hadn't expected it to last. She didn't blame me at all. I wish to God she had now. Perhaps I'd feel better about it.

Inspector She had to move out of those rooms?

Gerald Yes, we'd agreed about that. She's saved a little money during the summer—she'd lived very economically on what I'd allowed her—and didn't want to take any more from me, but I insisted on a parting gift of enough money—though it wasn't so very much—to see her through to the end of the year.

Inspector Did she tell you what she proposed to do after you'd left her?

Gerald No. She refused to talk about that. I got the idea, once or twice from what she said, that she thought of leaving Brumley. Whether she did or not—I don't know. Did she?

Inspector (*moving up* L. *of the table to the sideboard*) Yes. She went away for about two months. To some seaside place.

Gerald By herself?

Inspector Yes. I think she went away—to be alone, to be quiet, to remember all that had happened between you.

Gerald How do you know that?

Inspector She kept a rough sort of diary. And she said there that she had to go away and be quiet and remember "just to make it last longer". She felt there'd never be anything as good again for her—so she had to make it last longer.

Gerald (*gravely*) I see. Well, I never saw her again, and that's all I can tell you.

Inspector It's all I want to know from you.

Gerald In that case—as I'm rather more—upset—by this business than I probably appear to be—and—well, I'd like to be alone for a little while —I'd be glad if you'd let me go.

Inspector Go where? Home?

Gerald No. I'll just go out—walk about—for a while, if you don't mind. I'll come back. (*He turns to the door*)

Inspector All right, Mr Croft.

Sheila (*rising and crossing to Gerald*) But just in case you forget—or decide not to come back, Gerald, I think you'd better take this with you. (*She hands him the ring*)

Gerald I see. Well, I was expecting this.

Sheila I don't dislike you as I did half-an-hour ago, Gerald. In fact, in some odd way, I rather respect you more than I've ever done before. I knew anyhow you were lying about those months last year when you hardly came near me. I knew there was something fishy about that time. And now at least you've been honest. And I believe what you told us about the way you helped her at first. Just out of pity. And it was my fault really that she was so desperate when you first met her. But this has made a difference. You and I aren't the same people who sat down to dinner here. We'd have to start all over again, getting to know each other—

Birling (*crossing towards Sheila, below the table*) Now, Sheila, I'm not defending him. But you must understand that a lot of young men—

Sheila Don't interfere, please, Father. Gerald knows what I mean, and you apparently don't.

Birling turns back to the fire

Gerald Yes, I know what you mean. But I'm coming back—if I may.

Sheila All right. (*She sits* L. *of the table*)

Mrs Birling (*moving* C. *below the table*) Well, really, I don't know. I think we've just about come to the end of this wretched business—

Gerald I don't think so. Excuse me.

He goes out

Birling crosses up stage to the door to follow him, but as he reaches the door the front door slams off stage. Mrs Birling sits below the table

Sheila (*to the Inspector*) You know, you never showed him that photograph of her.

Inspector No, it wasn't necessary.

Mrs Birling You have a photograph of the girl?

Inspector Yes, I think you'd better look at it. (*He comes round* R. *of the table to Mrs Birling*)

Mrs Birling I don't see any particular reason why I should—

Inspector Probably not. But you'd better look at it.

Mrs Birling Very well.

The Inspector produces the photograph and Mrs Birling looks hard at it

Inspector (*taking back the photograph*) You recognize her?

Mrs Birling No. Why should I?

Inspector Of course she might have changed lately, but I can't believe she could have changed so much.

Mrs Birling I don't understand you, Inspector.

Inspector (*moving to the fireplace*) You mean you don't choose to, Mrs Birling.

Mrs Birling (*angrily*) I meant what I said.

Inspector You're not telling me the truth.

Mrs Birling (*rising*) I beg your pardon!

Birling (*crossing to the table* L. *of Mrs Birling; angrily to the Inspector*) Look here, I'm not going to have this, Inspector. You'll apologize at once.

Inspector Apologize for what—doing my duty?

Birling No, for being so offensive about it. I'm a public man—

Inspector (*massively*) Public men, Mr Birling, have responsibilities as well as privileges.

Birling Possibly. But you weren't asked to come here to talk to me about my responsibilities.

Sheila Let's hope not. Though I'm beginning to wonder.

Mrs Birling Does that mean anything, Sheila?

Sheila (*rising*) It means that we've no excuses now for putting on airs and that if we've any sense we won't try. Father threw this girl out because she asked for decent wages. I went and pushed her further out, right into the street, just because I was angry and she was pretty. Gerald set her up as his mistress and then dropped her when it suited him. And now you're pretending you don't recognize her from that photograph. I admit I don't know why you should, but I know jolly well you did in fact recognize her, from the way you looked. And if you're not telling the truth, why should the Inspector apologize? And can't you see, both of you, you're making it worse?

We hear the front door slam

Birling That was the door again.

Mrs Birling Gerald must have come back.

Inspector Unless your son has just gone out.

Birling I'll see.

He turns to the door and goes out quickly

The Inspector turns to Mrs Birling

Inspector Mrs Birling, you're a member—a prominent member—of the Brumley Women's Charity Organization, aren't you?

Mrs Birling sits below the table. She does not reply

Sheila Go on, Mother. You might as well admit it. (*To the Inspector*) Yes, she is. Why? (*She sits* L. *of the table*)

Inspector (*crossing down stage to the desk; calmly*) It's an organization to which women in distress can appeal for help in various forms. Isn't that so?

Mrs Birling (*with dignity*) Yes. We've done a great deal of useful work in helping deserving cases.

Inspector There was a meeting of the interviewing Committee two weeks ago?

Mrs Birling I dare say there was.

Inspector You know very well there was, Mrs Birling. You were in the chair?

Mrs Birling And if I was, what business is it of yours?

Inspector (*severely*) Do you want me to tell you—in plain words?

Birling enters. He is looking rather agitated. He closes the door

Birling That must have been Eric.

Mrs Birling (*alarmed*) Have you been up to his room?

Birling Yes. And I called out on both landings. It must have been Eric we heard go out then.

Mrs Birling Silly boy! Where can he have gone to?

Birling I can't imagine. But he was in one of his excitable queer moods, and even though we don't need him here—

Inspector (*cutting in, sharply*) We do need him here. And if he's not back soon, I shall have to go and find him.

Birling and Mrs Birling exchange bewildered and rather frightened glances

Sheila (*rising and crossing above the table to the fireplace*) He's probably just gone to cool off. He'll be back soon.

Inspector (*severely*) I hope so.

Mrs Birling And why should you hope so?

Inspector (*crossing to* L. *of Mrs Birling*) I'll explain why when you've answered my questions, Mrs Birling.

Birling Is there any reason why my wife should answer questions from you, Inspector?

Inspector Yes, a very good reason. You'll remember that Mr Croft told us—quite truthfully, I believe—that he hadn't spoken to or seen Eva Smith since last September. But Mrs Birling spoke to and saw her only two weeks ago.

Sheila (*astonished*) Mother!

Birling Is this true?

Mrs Birling (*after a pause*) Yes, quite true.

Sheila sits in the armchair

Inspector She appealed to your organization for help?
Mrs Birling Yes.
Inspector Not as Eva Smith?
Mrs Birling No. Nor as Daisy Renton.
Inspector As what then?
Mrs Birling First, she called herself Mrs Birling—
Birling (*astounded*) *Mrs Birling!*
Mrs Birling Yes. I think it was simply a piece of gross impertinence—
quite deliberate—and naturally that was one of the things that prejudiced
me against her case.
Birling (*crossing up to the sideboard*) And I should think so! Damned
impudence! (*He pours himself a drink*)
Inspector You admit being prejudiced against her case?
Mrs Birling Yes.
Sheila Mother, she's just died a horrible death—don't forget.

The Inspector moves up L., *above the chair* L. *of the table*

Mrs Birling I'm very sorry. But I think she had only herself to blame.
Inspector Was it owing to your influence, as the most prominent member
of the Committee, that help was refused the girl?
Mrs Birling Possibly.
Inspector Was it or was it not your influence?

Birling moves down to the fireplace

Mrs Birling (*rising and moving away to* R.; *stung*) Yes, it was. I didn't like
her manner. She'd impertinently made use of our name, though she
pretended afterwards it just happened to be the first she thought of. She
had to admit, after I began questioning her, that she had no claim to the
name, that she wasn't married, and that the story she told at first—
about a husband who'd deserted her—was quite false. It didn't take me
long to get the truth—or some of the truth—out of her.
Inspector Why did she ask for help?
Mrs Birling (*moving up to the* R. *end of the sideboard*) You know very well
why she asked for help.
Inspector No, I don't. I know why she *needed* help. But as I wasn't there,
I don't know what she asked it for from your committee.
Mrs Birling I don't think we need discuss it.
Inspector You have no hope of *not* discussing it, Mrs Birling.
Mrs Birling (*turning on the Inspector*) If you think you can bring any
pressure to bear upon me, Inspector, you're quite mistaken. Unlike the
other three, I did nothing I'm ashamed of or that won't bear investiga-
tion. The girl asked for assistance. We are asked to look carefully into
the claims made upon us. I wasn't satisfied with this girl's claim—she
seemed to me to be not a good case—and so I used my influence to have
it refused. And in spite of what's happened to the girl since, I consider

I did my duty. (*As she moves to the fireplace up stage of Mr Birling*) So if I prefer not to discuss it any further, you have no power to make me change my mind.

Inspector Yes I have.

Mrs Birling (*turning to face the Inspector*) No you haven't. Simply because I've done nothing wrong—and you know it.

Inspector (*very deliberately*) I think you did something terribly wrong—and that you're going to spend the rest of your life regretting it. I wish you'd been with me tonight in the Infirmary. You'd have seen—

Sheila (*bursting in*) No, no, please! Not that again. I've imagined it enough already.

Inspector (*very deliberately*) Then the next time you imagine it, just remember that this girl was going to have a child.

Sheila (*horrified*) No! Oh—horrible—horrible! How could she have wanted to kill herself.

Inspector Because she'd been turned out and turned down too many times. This was the end.

Sheila Mother, you must have known.

Inspector It was because she was going to have a child that she went for assistance to your mother's Committee.

Birling Look here, this wasn't Gerald Croft—

Inspector (*cutting in, sharply*) No, no. Nothing to do with him.

Sheila Thank goodness for that! Though I don't know why I should care now.

Inspector (*to Mrs Birling*) And you've nothing further to tell me, eh?

Mrs Birling I'll tell you what I told her. Go and look for the father of the child. It's his responsibility.

Inspector That doesn't make it any the less yours. She came to you for help, at a time when no woman could have needed it more. And you not only refused it yourself but saw to it that the others refused it too. She was here alone, almost penniless, desperate. She needed not only money but advice, sympathy, friendliness. You've had children. You must have known what she was feeling. And you slammed the door in her face.

Sheila (*with feeling*) Mother, I think it was cruel and vile.

Birling (*dubiously*) I must say, Sybil, that when this comes out at the inquest, it isn't going to do us much good. The Press might easily take it up—

Mrs Birling (*agitated now*) Oh, stop it, both of you. And please remember before you start accusing me of anything again that it wasn't I who had her turned out of her employment—which probably began it all. (*She turns to the Inspector, moves to the chair below the table and sits*)

Birling sits in the chair from R. of the table

In the circumstances I think I was justified. The girl had begun by telling us a pack of lies. Afterwards, when I got at the truth, I discovered that she knew who the father was, she was quite certain about that, and so I told her it was her business to make him responsible. If he refused to marry her—and in my opinion he ought to be compelled to—then he must at least support her.

Inspector And what did she reply to that?

Mrs Birling (*rising and crossing down* L.) Oh—a lot of silly nonsense.

Inspector What was it?

Mrs Birling (*moving to the desk*) Whatever it was, I know it made me finally lose all patience with her. She was giving herself ridiculous airs. She was claiming elaborate fine feelings and scruples that were simply absurd in a girl of her position.

Inspector (*very sternly*) Her position now is that she lies with a burnt-out inside on a slab.

Birling rises and tries to protest

(*He turns on Birling*) Don't stammer and yammer at me again, man. I'm losing all patience with you people. *What did she say?*

Mrs Birling (*rather cowed*) She said that the father was only a youngster—silly and wild and drinking too much. There couldn't be any question of marrying him—it would be wrong for them both. He had given her money but she didn't want to take any more money from him.

Inspector Why didn't she want to take any more money from him?

Mrs Birling (*crossing to the fireplace*) All a lot of nonsense—I didn't believe a word of it.

Inspector I'm not asking you if you believed it. I want to know what she said. Why didn't she want to take any more money from this boy?

Mrs Birling Oh—she had some fancy reason. As if a girl of that sort would ever refuse money!

Inspector (*moving below the table towards Mrs Birling; sternly*) I warn you, you're making it worse for yourself. What reason did she give for not taking any more money?

Mrs Birling Her story was—that he'd said something one night, when he was drunk, that gave her the idea that it wasn't his money.

Inspector Where had he got it from then?

Mrs Birling He'd stolen it.

Inspector (*turning and moving slowly* L.) So she'd come to you for assistance because she didn't want to take stolen money?

Mrs Birling That's the story she finally told, after I'd refused to believe her original story—that she was a married woman who'd been deserted by her husband. I didn't see any reason to believe that one story should be any truer than the other. Therefore, you're quite wrong to suppose I shall regret what I did. (*She sits below the table*)

Inspector (*turning to Mrs Birling*) But if her story was true, if this boy had been giving her stolen money, then she came to you for help because she wanted to keep this youngster out of any more trouble—isn't that so?

Mrs Birling Possibly. But it sounded ridiculous to me. So I was perfectly justified in advising my Committee not to allow her claim for assistance.

Inspector You're not even sorry now, when you know what happened to the girl?

Mrs Birling I'm sorry she should have come to such a horrible end. But I accept no blame for it at all.

Inspector Who is to blame then?

Mrs Birling First the girl herself.

Sheila (*bitterly*) For letting Father and me have her chucked out of her jobs?

Mrs Birling Secondly, I blame the young man who was the father of the child she was going to have. If, as she said, he didn't belong to her class, and was some drunken young idler, then that's all the more reason why he shouldn't escape. He should be made an example of. If the girl's death is due to anybody, then it's due to him.

Inspector And if her story is true—that he was stealing money—

Mrs Birling (*rather agitated now*) There's no point in assuming that—

Inspector But supposing we do, what then?

Mrs Birling Then he'd be entirely responsible—because the girl wouldn't have come to us, and have been refused assistance, if it hadn't been for him—

Inspector So he's the chief culprit anyhow?

Mrs Birling Certainly. And he ought to be dealt with very severely—

Sheila (*rising and crossing to Mrs Birling; with sudden alarm*) Mother—stop—stop.

Birling Be quiet, Sheila!

Sheila But don't you see—

Mrs Birling (*severely*) You're behaving like a hysterical child tonight.

Sheila moves up R. *of the table*

(*She turns to the Inspector*) And if you'd take some steps to find this young man and then make sure that he's compelled to confess in public his responsibility—instead of staying here asking quite unnecessary questions—then you really would be doing your duty.

Inspector (*grimly*) Don't worry, Mrs Birling. I shall do my duty! (*He looks at his watch*)

Mrs Birling (*triumphantly*) I'm glad to hear it.

Inspector No hushing up, eh? Make an example of the young man, eh? Public confession of responsibility—um?

Mrs Birling Certainly. I consider it your duty. (*She rises*) And now no doubt you'd like to say goodnight.

Inspector Not yet. I'm waiting. (*He moves to the chair* L. *of the table and sits*)

Mrs Birling Waiting for what?

Inspector To do my duty.

Sheila (*coming down* R. *to Mrs Birling; distressed*) Now, Mother—don't you see? (*She turns to Birling and buries her face against his shoulder, crying*)

Mrs Birling and Birling exchange frightened glances

Birling (*terrified now*) Look Inspector, you're not trying to tell us that—that my boy—is mixed up in this—?

Inspector (*sternly*) If he is, then we know what to do, don't we? Mrs
  Birling has just told us.

Birling (*crossing to Mrs Birling; thunderstruck*) My God! By—look here—

Mrs Birling (*agitatedly*) I don't believe it. I *won't* believe it . . . (*She sits
  below the table*)

Sheila (*moving below Mrs Birling and kneeling*) Mother—I begged and
  begged you to stop—

*The Inspector holds up a hand. We hear the front door. The Inspector rises
and turns to face the door. They all wait, looking towards the door*

  Eric enters, looking extremely pale and distressed

He meets their enquiring stares. There is a little cry from Mrs Birling as—

the CURTAIN *falls quickly*

ACT III

The same. The action is continuous

When the CURTAIN *rises, Eric is just entering. The others are staring at him.*

Eric You know, don't you?

Inspector (*gravely*) Yes we know. (*He moves up to the sideboard*)

Eric shuts the door and comes further into the room

Mrs Birling (*distressed*) Eric, I can't believe it. There must be some mistake. You don't know what we've been saying.

Sheila (*rising and crossing to the armchair*) It's a good job for him he doesn't, isn't it?

Eric Why?

Sheila Because Mother's been busy blaming everything on the young man who got this girl into trouble, and saying he shouldn't escape and should be made an example of—

Birling That's enough, Sheila.

Eric (*bitterly*) You haven't made it any easier for me, have you, Mother?

Mrs Birling But I didn't know it was *you*—I never dreamt. Besides, you're not that type—you don't get drunk—

Sheila Of course he does. I told you he did. (*She sits in the armchair*)

Eric *You* told her. Why, you little sneak!

Sheila No, that's not fair, Eric. I could have told her months ago, but of course I didn't. I only told her tonight because I knew everything was coming out—it was simply bound to come out tonight—so I thought she might as well know in advance. Don't forget—I've already been through it.

Mrs Birling Sheila, I simply don't understand your attitude. (*She rises and crosses* R. *to the chair from* R. *of the table, in which she sits*)

Birling Neither do I. If you'd had any sense of loyalty—

Inspector (*coming down* R. *of the table; cutting in, smoothly*) Just a minute Mr Birling. There'll be plenty of time to adjust your family relationships when I've gone. But now I must hear what your son has to tell me. (*Sternly to the three of them*) And I'll be obliged if you'll let us get on without any further interruptions. (*Turning to Eric*) Now then.

Eric (*miserably*) Could I have a drink first?

Birling (*explosively*) No!

Inspector (*firmly*) Yes. (*As Birling looks like interrupting explosively*) I know—he's your son and this is your house—but look at him. He needs a drink now just to see him through.

Birling (*to Eric*) All right. Go on.

Eric goes up to the sideboard and pours himself out a whisky. His whole manner of handling the decanter and then the drink shows his familiarity with quick heavy drinking. The others watch him narrowly

(*Bitterly*) I understand a lot of things now I didn't understand before.

Eric comes down to the table, above the chair, L. of it

Inspector Don't start on that. I want to get on. (*To Eric*) When did you first meet this girl?
Eric One night last November.
Inspector Where did you meet her?
Eric In the Palace bar. I'd been there an hour or so with two or three chaps. I was a bit squiffy. (*He sits L. of table*)
Inspector What happened then?
Eric I began talking to her, and stood her a few drinks. I was rather far gone by the time we had to go.
Inspector Was she drunk too?
Eric She told me afterwards that she was a bit, chiefly because she'd not had much to eat that day.
Inspector Had she gone there—to solicit?
Eric No, she hadn't. She wasn't that sort really. But—well, I suppose she didn't know what to do. There was some woman who wanted her to go there. I never quite understood about that.
Inspector You went with her to her lodgings that night?
Eric Yes, I insisted—it seems. I'm not very clear about it, but afterwards she told me she didn't want me to go in but that—well, I was in that state when a chap easily turns nasty—and I threatened to make a row.
Inspector So she let you in?
Eric Yes. And that's when it happened. And I didn't even remember—that's the hellish thing. How stupid it all is!
Mrs Birling (*rising; with a cry*) Oh—Eric—how could you?
Birling (*sharply*) Sheila, take your mother along to the drawing-room—
Sheila (*protesting*) But—I want to—
Birling (*very sharply*) You heard what I said. (*Gentler*) Go on, Sybil.

He leads Mrs Birling across to the door

   Sheila rises and follows, and takes Mrs Birling out

Birling shuts the door

Inspector When did you meet her again?
Eric (*rising and moving above the table to R.*) About a fortnight afterwards.
Inspector By appointment?
Eric No. And I couldn't remember her name or where she lived. It was all very vague. But I happened to see her again in the Palace bar.
Inspector More drinks?
Eric Yes, though that time I wasn't so bad.
Inspector But you took her home again?
Eric (*coming down to the fireplace*) Yes. And this time we talked a bit. She

told me something about herself and I talked too. Told her my name and what I did.

Inspector And you made love again?

Eric Yes. I wasn't in love with her or anything—but I liked her—she was pretty and a good sport—

Birling (*moving* L.C.; *harshly*) So you had to go to bed with her?

Eric Well, I'm old enough to be married, aren't I, and I'm not married, and I hate these fat old tarts round the town—the ones I see some of your respectable friends with—

Birling (*angrily*) I don't want any of that talk from you—

Inspector (*moving below the table to* C.; *very sharply*) I don't want any of it from either of you. Settle it afterwards.

Birling sits L. *of the table*

(*To Eric*) Did you arrange to see each other after that?

Eric Yes. And the next time—or the time after that—she told me she thought she was going to have a baby.

Inspector And of course she was very worried about it?

Eric Yes, and so was I. I was in a hell of a state about it.

Inspector Did she suggest that you ought to marry her?

Eric No. She didn't want me to marry her. (*He comes down to the armchair*) Said I didn't love her—and all that. In a way, she treated me—as if I were a kid. Though I was nearly as old as she was.

Inspector So what did you propose to do?

Eric Well, she hadn't a job—and didn't feel like trying again for one—and she'd no money left—so I insisted on giving her enough money to keep her going—until she refused to take any more—

Inspector How much did you give her altogether?

Eric I suppose—about fifty pounds all told.

Birling (*rising and crossing below the table to Eric*) Fifty pounds—on top of drinking and going round the town! Where did you get fifty pounds from?

Eric does not reply

Inspector (*moving to Eric*) That's my question too.

Eric (*miserably*) I got it—from the office—

Birling *My* office?

The Inspector moves up R. *of the table*

Eric (*sitting in the armchair*) Yes.

Inspector You mean—you stole the money?

Eric Not really.

Birling (*angrily*) What do you mean—*not really*?

Mrs Birling and Sheila enter. Eric does not reply

Sheila (*turning down to the desk*) This isn't my fault.

Mrs Birling (*to Birling*) I'm sorry, Arthur, but I simply couldn't stay in there. I had to know what's happening.

Birling (*savagely*) Well, I can tell you what's happening. He's admitted he was responsible for the girl's condition, and now he's telling us he supplied her with money he stole from the office.

Mrs Birling (*shocked*) Eric! You stole money? (*She comes below the table*)

Eric No, not really. I intended to pay it back.

Birling We've heard that story before. How could you have paid it back?

Eric I'd have managed somehow. I had to have some money—

Birling I don't understand how you could take as much as that out of the office without somebody knowing.

Eric There were some small accounts to collect, and I asked for cash—

Birling Gave the firm's receipt and then kept the money, eh?

Eric Yes.

Birling You must give me a list of those accounts. I've got to cover this up as soon as I can. You damned fool—why didn't you come to me when you found yourself in this mess?

Mrs Birling sits below the table

Eric Because you're not the kind of father a chap could go to when he's in trouble—that's why.

Birling (*angrily*) Don't talk to me like that. Your trouble is—you've been spoilt—

Inspector (*coming down* R. *of the table and crossing* C. *to* L. *of Mrs Birling; cutting in*) And my trouble is—that I haven't much time. You'll be able to divide the responsibility between you when I've gone.

Birling breaks to the fireplace

(*To Eric*) Just one last question, that's all. The girl discovered that this money you were giving her was stolen, didn't she?

Eric (*miserably*) Yes. That was the worst of all. She wouldn't have any more, and she didn't want to see me again. (*In a sudden startled tone*) Here, but how did you know that? Did she tell you?

Inspector (*crossing up to the table* R. *of Mrs Birling*) No. She told me nothing. I never spoke to her.

Sheila She told Mother.

Mrs Birling (*alarmed*) Sheila!

Sheila Well, he has to know.

Eric (*rising and moving a step to* L.; *to Mrs Birling*) She told you? Did she come here—but then she couldn't have done, she didn't even know I lived here. What happened?

Mrs Birling, distressed, shakes her head but does not reply

(*He crosses to Mrs Birling*) Come on, don't just look like that. Tell me— tell me—what happened?

Inspector (*with calm authority*) I'll tell you. She went to your mother's committee for help, after she'd done with you. Your mother refused that help.

Eric (*nearly at breaking point*) Then—you killed her. She came to you to protect me—and you turned her away—yes, and you killed her—and

the child she'd have had too—my child—your own grandchild—you
killed them both—damn you, damn you—(*He breaks away down* R.)
Mrs Birling (*rising; very distressed now*) No—Eric—please—I didn't
know—I didn't understand—
Eric (*crossing to Mrs Birling; almost threatening her*) You don't understand anything. You never did. You never even tried—you—
Sheila (*frightened*) Eric, don't—don't—

Birling comes down, catches Eric by the arm and pushes him down R.

Birling (*furious, intervening*) Why, you hysterical young fool—get back—
or I'll—
Inspector (*taking charge, masterfully*) Stop!

They are suddenly quiet, staring at him

And be quiet for a moment and listen to me. I don't need to know any
more. Neither do you. This girl killed herself—and died a horrible
death. But each of you helped to kill her. Remember that. Never forget
it. (*He looks from one to the other of them carefully*) But then I don't
think you ever will. Remember what you did, Mrs Birling. You turned
her away when she most needed help. You refused her even the pitiable
little bit of organized charity you had in your power to grant her.

Mrs Birling moves away and sits L. *of the table*

(*To Eric*) Remember what you did—
Eric (*sitting in the armchair; unhappily*) My God—I'm not likely to forget.
Inspector Just used her for the end of a stupid drunken evening, as if she
were an animal, a thing, not a person. No, you won't forget. (*He looks
at Sheila*)
Sheila (*crossing to the Inspector; bitterly*). I know. I had her turned out
of a job. I started it.
Inspector You helped—but didn't start it.

Sheila sits below the table

(*Rather savagely to Birling*) You started it. She wanted twenty-five
shillings a week instead of twenty-two and sixpence. You made her pay
a heavy price for that. And now she'll make you pay a heavier price still.
Birling (*unhappily*) Look, Inspector—I'd give thousands—yes, thousands—
Inspector You're offering the money at the wrong time, Mr Birling.

Birling sits in the chair from R. *of the table*

(*He makes a move as if concluding the session. He surveys them sar-
donically. Then he domes down* C.) No, I don't think any of you will
forget. Nor that young man, Croft, though he at least had some affection
for her and made her happy for a time. (*He turns up stage to face them*)
Well, Eva Smith's gone. You can't do her any more harm. And you
can't do her any good now either. You can't even say, "I'm sorry, Eva
Smith." (*He crosses to the door*)
Sheila (*crying quietly*) That's the worst of it.

Inspector (*turning at the door*) But just remember this. One Eva Smith has gone—but there are millions and millions and millions of Eva Smiths and John Smiths still left with us, with their lives, their hopes and fears, their suffering and chance of happiness, all intertwined with our lives, with what we think and say and do. We don't live alone. We are members of one body. We are responsible for each other. And I tell you that the time will soon come when, if men will not learn that lesson, then they will be taught it in fire and blood and anguish. Goodnight.

He walks straight out, leaving them staring, subdued and wondering

Sheila is still quietly crying. Mrs Birling has collapsed into a chair. Eric is brooding desperately. Birling, the only active one, hears the front door slam, rises, moves hesitatingly towards the door, stops, and looks gloomily at the other three

Birling (*angrily to Eric*) You're the one I blame for this.

Eric I'll bet I am.

Birling (*angrily*) Yes, and you don't realize yet all you've done. Most of this is bound to come out. There'll be a public scandal. (*He moves towards the sideboard*)

Eric Well, I don't care now.

Birling (*stopping*) You! You don't seem to care about anything. But I care. I was almost certain for a knighthood in the next honours' list—

Eric rises and moves to the fire. He laughs rather hysterically, pointing at Birling

Eric (*laughing*) Oh—for God's sake! What does it matter now whether they give you a knighthood or not?

Birling (*stormily*) It doesn't matter to you. Apparently nothing matters to you. But it may interest you to know that until every penny of that money you stole is repaid, you'll work for nothing. And there's going to be no more of this drinking round the town—and picking up women in the Palace bar—(*He moves to the sideboard and pours out a whisky*)

Mrs Birling (*coming to life*) I should think not. Eric, I'm absolutely ashamed of you.

Eric Well, I don't blame you. But don't forget I'm ashamed of you as well—yes, both of you.

Birling (*coming down to the back of Mrs Birling's chair; angrily*) Drop that. There's every excuse for what both your mother and I did—it turned out unfortunately, that's all—

Sheila (*scornfully*) That's all.

Birling Well, what have you to say?

Sheila I don't know where to begin.

Birling Then don't begin. Nobody wants you to.

Sheila I behaved badly, too. I know I did. I'm ashamed of myself. But now you're beginning all over again to pretend that nothing much has happened—

Birling Nothing much has happened! Haven't I already said there'll be a public scandal—unless we're lucky—and who here will suffer from that more than I will?

Sheila But that's not what I'm talking about. I don't care about that. The point is, you don't seem to have learnt anything.

Birling Didn't I? Well, you're quite wrong there. I learnt plenty tonight. And you don't want me to tell you what I've learnt, I hope. When I look back on tonight—when I think of what I was feeling when the five of us sat down to dinner at that table—

Eric (*cutting in*) Yes, and do you remember what you said to Gerald and me after dinner, when you were feeling so pleased with yourself? You told us that a man has to make his own way, look after himself and mind his own business, and that we weren't to take any notice of these cranks who tell us that everybody has to look after everybody else, as if we were all mixed up together. Do you remember? Yes—and then one of those cranks walked in—the Inspector. (*He laughs bitterly*) I didn't notice you told him that it's every man for himself. (*He turns to the fire*)

Sheila (*sharply attentive*) Is that when the Inspector came, just after father had said that? (*She rises and moves* R. *of the table towards Eric*)

Eric Yes. What of it?

Mrs Birling Now what's the matter, Sheila?

Sheila (*slowly*) It's queer—very queer—(*She turns and looks at them reflectively*)

Mrs Birling (*with some excitement*) I know what you're going to say. Because I've been wondering myself.

Sheila It doesn't much matter now, of course—but *was* he really a Police Inspector?

Birling Well, if he wasn't, it matters a devil of a lot. Makes all the difference.

Sheila Well, it doesn't to me. And it oughtn't to you, either.

Mrs Birling Don't be childish, Sheila.

Sheila (*flaring up*) I'm not being. If you want to know, it's you two who are being childish—trying not to face the facts.

Birling I won't have that sort of talk. Any more of that and you leave this room.

Eric That'll be terrible for her, won't it?

Sheila I'm going anyhow in a minute or two. But don't you see, if all that's come out tonight is true, then it doesn't much matter who it was who made us confess. And it *was* true, wasn't it? That's what's important—and not whether a man is a Police Inspector or not.

Eric He was our Police Inspector all right. (*He moves above the table*)

Sheila That's what I mean, Eric. (*Turning to her parents*) But if it's any comfort to you—and it isn't to me—I have an idea—and I had it all along vaguely—that there was something curious about him. He never seemed like an ordinary Police Inspector—

Birling (*rather excited*) You're right. I felt it too. (*To Mrs Birling*) Didn't you?

Mrs Birling Well, I must say his manner was quite extraordinary. So—rude—and assertive—

Eric sits R. *above the table*

Birling (*crossing to the desk*) Then look at the way he talked to me. Telling me to shut up—and so on. He must have known I was an ex-Lord Mayor and a magistrate and so forth. (*He turns*) Besides—the way he talked—you remember. I mean, they don't *talk* like that. I've had dealings with dozens of them.

Sheila (*slowly*) You know, we hardly ever told him anything he didn't know. Did you notice that?

Birling (*sitting at the desk*) That's nothing. He had a bit of information, left by the girl, and made a few smart guesses—but the fact remains that if we hadn't talked so much, he'd have had little to go on. (*He looks angrily at them*) And really, when I come to think of it, why you all had to go letting everything come out like that, beats me.

Sheila It's all right talking like that now. But he made us confess. (*She moves up to the sideboard*)

Mrs Birling He certainly didn't make me *confess*—as you call it. I told him quite plainly that I thought I had done no more than my duty.

Sheila Oh—Mother!

Birling The fact is, you allowed yourselves to be bluffed. Yes—bluffed.

Mrs Birling (*protesting*) Now, really—Arthur.

Birling No, not you, my dear. But these two. That fellow obviously didn't like us. He was prejudiced from the start. Probably a Socialist or some sort of crank—he talked like one. And then, instead of standing up to him, you let him bluff you into talking about your private affairs. You ought to have stood up to him.

Eric (*rising and moving* R. *of the table; sulkily*) Well, I didn't notice you standing up to him.

Birling No, because by that time you'd admitted you'd been taking money. What chance had I after that? I was a fool not to have insisted upon seeing him alone.

Eric That wouldn't have worked.

Sheila Of course it wouldn't.

Mrs Birling Really, from the way you children talk, you might be wanting to help him instead of us. (*She rises and comes down to Birling*) Now just be quiet so that your father can decide what we ought to do. (*She looks expectantly at Birling*)

Birling (*rising and moving below the table to* C.*; dubiously*) Yes—well. We'll have to do something—and get to work quickly too.

There is a ring at the front door. Birling stops. They all look at each other in alarm

Now who's this? Had I better go?

Mrs Birling No. Edna'll go. I asked her to wait up to make us some tea.

Sheila (*coming down to* L. *of the table*) It might be Gerald coming back.

Mrs Birling sits at the desk

Birling (*sitting below the table; relieved*) Yes, of course. I'd forgotten about him.

Edna enters

Edna It's Mr Croft.

Gerald enters. He crosses below Sheila to L.C.

Edna goes out

Gerald I hope you don't mind my coming back?

Mrs Birling No, of course not, Gerald.

Gerald I had a special reason for coming back. (*He moves* C.) When did that Inspector go?

Sheila (*coming down to* L. *of Gerald*) Only a few minutes ago. He put us all through it—

Mrs Birling (*warningly*) Sheila!

Sheila Gerald might as well know.

Birling (*hastily*) Now—now—we needn't bother him with all that stuff.

Sheila All right. (*To Gerald*) But we're all in it—up to the neck. It got worse after you left.

Gerald How did he behave?

Sheila He was frightening.

Birling If you ask me, he behaved in a very peculiar and suspicious manner.

Mrs Birling The rude way he spoke to Mr Birling and me—it was quite extraordinary! Why?

They all look enquiringly at Gerald

Birling (*excitedly*) You know something. What is it?

Gerald (*slowly*) That man wasn't a police officer.

Sheila sits L. *of the table*

Birling (*astounded*) What?

Mrs Birling Are you certain?

Gerald I'm almost certain. That's what I came back to tell you.

Birling (*excitedly*) Good lad! You asked about him, eh?

Gerald Yes. I met a police sergeant I know down the road. I asked him about the Inspector Goole and described the chap carefully to him. He swore there wasn't any Inspector Goole or anybody like him on the force here.

Birling (*excitedly*) By jingo! A fake!

Mrs Birling (*rising and moving to* L. *of Sheila; triumphantly*) Didn't I tell you? Didn't I say I couldn't imagine a real police inspector talking like that to us?

Gerald Well, you were right. There isn't any such Inspector. We've been had.

Birling (*rising*) I'm going to make certain of this.

Mrs Birling What are you going to do?

Birling (*crossing to the telephone*) Ring up the Chief Constable—Colonel Roberts.

Mrs Birling (*coming below the table*) Careful what you say, dear. (*She sits below the table*)

Birling (*lifting the receiver*) Of course. (*Into the telephone*) Brumley eight-seven-five-two. (*To the others*) I was going to do this anyhow.

Eric moves up to the sideboard and pours himself out a whisky

I've had my suspicions all along. (*Into the telephone*) Colonel Roberts, please. Mr Arthur Birling here . . . Oh, Roberts—Birling here. Sorry to ring you up so late, but can you tell me if an Inspector Goole has joined your staff lately . . . Goole. G O O L E . . .

Eric comes down L. of the table

. . . a new man . . . (*He describes the appearance of the actor playing the part of the Inspector*) I see . . . yes . . . well, that settles it . . . No, just a little argument we were having here . . . Goodnight. (*He puts down the telephone and looks at the others*) There's no Inspector Goole on the police now. There's nobody who even looks like the man who came here. That man definitely wasn't a Police Inspector. As Gerald says— we've been had. (*He crosses to Mrs Birling*)

Mrs Birling (*rising and crossing to the fire*) I felt it all the time. He never talked like one. He never even looked like one.

Birling This makes a difference, y'know. In fact, it makes *all* the difference.

Sheila (*rising and moving to the desk; bitterly*) I suppose we're all nice people now.

Birling If you've nothing more sensible than that to say, Sheila, you'd better keep quiet.

Eric She's right, though.

Birling (*angrily*) And you'd better keep quiet anyhow. If that *had* been a Police Inspector and he'd heard you confess—

Mrs Birling (*warningly*) Arthur—careful!

Birling (*hastily*) Yes, yes.

Sheila (*moving down L.*) You see, Gerald, you're not allowed to know the rest of our crimes and idiocies.

Gerald (*crossing to Sheila*) That's all right, I don't want to. (*He turns to Birling*) What do you make of this business now? Was it a hoax?

Birling Of course. Somebody put that fellow up to coming here and hoaxing us. There are people in this town who dislike me enough to do that. We ought to have seen through it from the first. In the ordinary way, I believe I would have done. But coming like that, bang on top of our little celebration, just when we were all feeling so pleased with ourselves, naturally it took me by surprise.

Mrs Birling I wish I'd been here when that man first arrived. I'd have asked *him* a few questions before I allowed him to ask us any.

Gerald crosses to the armchair and sits

Sheila (*moving in to the table L. of the chair below it*) It's all right saying that now.

Mrs Birling I was the only one of you who didn't give in to him. And now I say we must discuss this business quietly and sensibly and decide if there's anything to be done about it.

Birling (*with hearty approval*) You're absolutely right, my dear. Already we've discovered one important fact—that that fellow was a fraud and we've been hoaxed—and that may not be the end of it by any means. (*He sits below the table*)

Gerald I'm sure it isn't.

Eric is moving restlessly down L.

Birling (*keenly interested*) You are, eh? Good! (*To Eric*) Eric, sit down.

Eric (*sulkily*) I'm all right.

Birling All right? You're anything but all right. And you needn't stand there—as if—as if—

Eric As if—what?

Birling As if you'd nothing to do with us. Just remember your own position, young man. If anybody's up to the neck in this business, you are, so you'd better take some interest in it.

Eric I do take some interest in it. I take too much, that's my trouble.

Sheila It's mine too.

Birling Now listen, you two. If you're still feeling on edge, then the least you can do is to keep quiet. Leave this to us. I'll admit that fellow's antics rattled us a bit. But we've found him out—and all we have to do is to keep our heads. Now it's our turn.

Sheila Our turn to do—what?

Mrs Birling (*sharply*) To behave sensibly, Sheila—which is more than you're doing.

Eric (*moving above the chair* L. *of the table; bursting out*) What's the use of talking about behaving sensibly. You're beginning to pretend now that nothing's really happened at all. And I can't see it like that. This girl's still dead, isn't she? Nobody's brought her to life have they?

Sheila (*eagerly*) That's just what I feel, Eric. And it's what they don't seem to understand.

Eric Whoever that chap was, the fact remains that I did what I did. And mother did what she did. And the rest of you did what you did to her. It's still the same rotten story whether it's been told to a Police Inspector or to somebody else. According to you, I ought to feel a lot better— (*He crosses to Gerald*) I stole some money, Gerald, you might as well know—

Birling rises and tries to interrupt

I don't care, let him know. The money's not the important thing. It's what happened to the girl and what we all did to her that matters. And I still feel the same about it, and that's why I don't feel like sitting down and having a nice cosy talk. (*He moves up* R. *of the table*)

Sheila And Eric's absolutely right. And it's the best thing any one of us has said tonight and it makes me feel a bit less ashamed of us. You're just beginning to pretend all over again.

Birling Look—for God's sake!

Mrs Birling (*protesting*) Arthur!

Birling Well, my dear, they're so damned exasperating. (*He sits again*) They just won't try to understand our position or to see the difference

between a lot of stuff like this coming out in private and a downright
public scandal.

Eric (*crossing above the table to* L.*; shouting*) And I say the girl's dead
and we all helped to kill her—and that's what matters—

Birling (*rising; shouting, threatening Eric*) And I say—either stop shouting
or get out. (*He glares at him. In a quieter tone*) Some fathers I know
would have kicked you out of the house anyhow by this time. So hold
your tongue if you want to stay here.

Eric (*coming down* L. *to the desk; quietly, bitterly*) I don't give a damn now
whether I stay here or not.

Birling (*crossing to Eric*) You'll stay here long enough to give me an
account of that money you stole—yes, and to pay it back too.

Sheila But that won't bring Eva Smith back to life, will it?

Eric And it doesn't alter the fact that we all helped to kill her.

Gerald (*rising*) But is it a fact?

Eric Of course it is. You don't know the whole story yet.

Sheila I suppose you're going to prove now you didn't spend last summer
keeping this girl instead of seeing me, eh?

Gerald I did keep a girl last summer. I've admitted it. And I'm sorry,
Sheila.

Sheila Well, I must admit you came out of it better than the rest of us.
The Inspector said that.

Birling (*moving up* L. *of the table to the sideboard; angrily*) He wasn't an
Inspector.

Sheila (*flaring up*) Well, he inspected us all right. And don't let's start
dodging and pretending now. Between us we drove that girl to commit
suicide.

Gerald Did we? (*He crosses to Sheila*) Who says so? Because I say—
there's no more real evidence we did than there was that that chap was
a Police Inspector.

Sheila Of course there is.

Gerald No there isn't. Look at it. A man comes here pretending to be a
police officer. It's a hoax of some kind. Now what does he do? Very
artfully, working on bits of information he's picked up here and there,
he bluffs us into confessing that we've all been mixed up in this girl's
life in one way or another.

Eric And so we have.

Gerald (*crossing to Eric*) But how do you know it's the same girl?

Birling (*coming down to the fireplace; eagerly*) Now wait a minute! Let's
see how that would work. Now—(*He hesitates*)—no, it wouldn't.

Eric We all admitted it.

Gerald All right, you all admitted something to do with a girl. But how
do you know it's the same girl? (*He looks round triumphantly at them*)

As they puzzle this out, Gerald turns to Birling

(*After a pause*) Look here, Mr Birling. You sack a girl called Eva Smith.
You've forgotten, but he shows you a photograph of her, and then you
remember. Right?

Birling Yes, that part's straightforward enough. But what then?

Gerald Well, then he happens to know that Sheila once had a girl sacked from Milwards shop. He tells us that it's this same Eva Smith. And he shows her a photograph that she recognizes.

Sheila Yes. The same photograph.

Gerald (*turning to Sheila*) How do you know it's the same photograph? Did you see the one your father looked at?

Sheila No, I didn't.

Gerald And did your father see the one he showed you?

Sheila No, he didn't. And I see what you mean now.

Gerald We've no proof it was the same photograph and therefore no proof it was the same girl. Now take me. I never saw a photograph, remember. He caught me out by suddenly announcing that this girl changed her name to Daisy Renton. I gave myself away at once because I'd known a Daisy Renton.

Birling (*eagerly*) And there wasn't the slightest proof that this Daisy Renton was really Eva Smith. We've only his word for it, and we'd his word for it that he was a Police Inspector and we know now he was lying. So he could have been lying all the time.

Gerald Of course he could. Probably was. Now what happened after I left?

Mrs Birling I was upset because Eric had left the house, and this man said that if Eric didn't come back, he'd have to go and find him. Well, that made me feel worse still. And his manner was so severe and he seemed so confident. Then quite suddenly he said Eva Smith had come to my committee for help only two weeks ago. And like a fool I said, yes she had.

Sheila But, Mother, don't forget that he showed you a photograph of the girl before that, and you obviously recognized it.

Gerald Did anybody else see it?

Mrs Birling No, he showed it only to me.

Gerald Then don't you see, there's still no proof it was really the same girl. He might have showed you the photograph of any girl who applied to the Committee. And how do we know she was really Eva Smith or Daisy Renton?

Birling Gerald's dead right. He could have used a different photograph each time and we'd be none the wiser. We may all have been recognizing different girls.

Gerald. Exactly. (*He crosses to Eric*) Did he ask you to identify a photograph, Eric?

Eric No. He didn't need a photograph by the time he'd got round to me. But obviously it must have been the girl I knew who went round to see mother.

Gerald Why must it?

Eric She said she had to have help because she wouldn't take any more stolen money. And the girl I knew had told me that already.

Gerald Even then, that may have been all nonsense.

Eric I don't see much nonsense about it when a girl goes and kills herself.

You lot may be letting yourselves out nicely, but I can't. Nor can mother. We did her in all right. (*He sits at the desk*)

Birling (*coming forward a step; eagerly*) Wait a minute, wait a minute. Don't be in such a hurry to put yourself into court. That interview with your mother could have been just as much a put-up job, like all the Police Inspector business. The whole damned thing can have been a piece of bluff.

Eric (*angrily*) How can it? The girl's dead, isn't she?

Gerald What girl? There were probably four or five different girls.

Eric (*rising*) That doesn't matter to me. The one I knew is dead.

Birling Is she? *How do we know she is?*

Gerald (*moving to* L. *of Sheila*) That's right. You've got it. How do we know any girl killed herself today?

Birling (*looking at Eric; triumphantly*) Now answer that one.

Eric sits at the desk

Let's look at it from this fellow's point of view. We're having a little celebration here and feeling rather pleased with ourselves. Now he has to work a trick on us. Well, the first thing he has to do is to give us such a shock that after that he can bluff us all the time. So he starts right off. A girl has just died in the Infirmary. She drank some strong disinfectant. Died in agony—

Eric All right, don't pile it on.

Birling (*triumphantly*) There you are, you see. Just repeating it shakes you a bit. And that's what he had to do. Shake us at once—and then start questioning us—until we didn't know where we were. Oh—let's admit that. He took us in all right. He had the laugh of us.

Eric He could laugh his head off—if I knew it really was a hoax.

Birling I'm convinced it is. No police enquiry. No one girl that all this happened to. No scandal—

Sheila And no suicide?

Gerald (*decisively*) We can settle that at once.

Sheila How?

Eric rises

Gerald By ringing up the Infirmary. Either there's a dead girl there or there isn't.

Birling (*uneasily*) It 'ud look a bit queer, wouldn't it—ringing up at this time of night—

Gerald (*crossing to the telephone*) I don't mind doing it.

Mrs Birling (*emphatically*) And if there isn't—

Gerald We'll see. (*He looks up the number*)

Birling moves to Mrs Birling. They all watch tensely

Brumley eight-nine-eight-six . . . Is that the Infirmary? This is Mr Gerald Croft—of Crofts Limited . . . Yes . . . we're rather worried about one of our employees. Have you had a girl brought in this afternoon

who committed suicide by drinking disinfectant—or any suicide? Yes, I'll wait. (*He waits*)

The others show their nervous tension. Eric rises and moves to Sheila. Birling wipes his brow, Sheila shivers, Eric clasps and unclasps his hands

Yes?... You're certain of that... I see. Well, thank you very much... Goodnight. (*He puts down the telephone and looks at them*) No girl has died in there today. They haven't had a suicide for months.

Birling (*triumphantly*) There you are! Proof positive. The whole story's just a lot of moonshine. Nothing but an elaborate sell! (*He produces a huge sigh of relief*) Nobody likes to be sold as badly as that—but—for all that—(*He smiles at them all. He moves up to the sideboard*) Gerald, have a drink.

Sheila sits below the table

Gerald (*smiling*) Thanks, I think I could just do with one now. (*He moves up to the fireplace*)

Birling (*pouring out two whiskies*) So could I.

Mrs Birling (*smiling*) And I must say, Gerald, you've argued this very cleverly, and I'm most grateful. (*She sits in the chair from* R. *of the table*)

Gerald Well, you see, while I was out of the house I'd time to cool off and think things out a little.

Birling comes down to the fireplace and gives Gerald a drink. Gerald sits in the armchair

Birling Yes, he didn't keep you on the run as he did the rest of us. I'll admit now he gave me a bit of a scare at the time. But I'd a special reason for not wanting any public scandal, just now. (*He raises his glass*) Well, here's to us. Come on, Sheila, don't look like that. All over now.

Sheila The worst part is. But you're forgetting one thing I still can't forget. Everything we said had happened really had happened. If it didn't end tragically, then that's lucky for us. But it might have done.

Birling (*jovially*) But the whole thing's different now. Come, come, you can see that, can't you? (*He imitates the Inspector in his final speech*) *You all helped to kill her.* (*Pointing at Sheila and Eric, and laughing*) And I wish you could have seen the look on your faces when he said that.

Sheila rises and moves towards the door

Sheila (*tensely*) I want to get out of this. It frightens me the way you talk.

Birling (*heartily*) Nonsense! You'll have a good laugh over it yet. Look, you'd better ask Gerald for that ring you gave back to him, hadn't you? Then you'll feel better.

Sheila (*passionately*) You're pretending everything's just as it was before.

Eric I'm not!

Sheila No, but these others are.

Birling Well, isn't it? We've been had, that's all.

Sheila So nothing really happened? So there's nothing to be sorry for, nothing to learn? We can all go on behaving just as we did?

Mrs Birling Well, why shouldn't we?

Sheila I tell you—whoever that Inspector was, it was anything but a joke. You knew it then. You began to learn something. And you've stopped now. You're ready to go on in the same old way.

Birling (*amused*) And you're not, eh?

Sheila No, because I remember what he said, how he looked, and what he made me feel. "Fire, blood and anguish!" And it frightens me the way you talk, and I can't listen to any more of it.

Eric I agree with Sheila, it frightens me too. (*He stands beside Sheila at the door*)

Birling Well, go to bed then, and don't stand there being hysterical.

Mrs Birling They're over-tired. In the morning they'll be as amused as we are.

Gerald (*rising and crossing to Sheila*) Everything's all right now, Sheila. (*He holds up the ring*) What about this ring?

Sheila No, not yet. It's too soon. I must think.

Birling (*pointing to Eric and Sheila*) Now look at the pair of them—the famous younger generation who know it all. And they can't even take a joke—

The telephone rings sharply. There is a moment's complete silence. Birling goes to answer it

Yes? . . . Mr Birling speaking . . . What?—Here?—

Gerald, Sheila and Eric move in to L. *of the table. Mrs Birling comes below the* R. *end of the table*

(*But obviously the other person has rung off. He puts the telephone down slowly and looks in a panic-stricken fashion at the others*) That was the police. A girl has just died—on her way to the Infirmary—after swallowing some disinfectant. And a Police Inspector is on his way here—to ask some—questions—

As they stare guiltily and dumbfounded—

the CURTAIN *falls*

FURNITURE AND PROPERTY LIST

ACT I

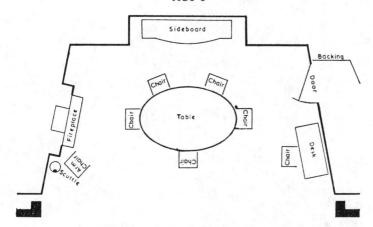

On stage: Dining table. *On it:* white table cloth, 2 silver candlesticks with shades, dish of fruit (centre piece), dish of nuts, nut-crackers, dish of sweets, matches in stand, box of cigarettes, 5 dessert plates, knives and forks, 5 finger bowls, 5 port glasses, 5 napkins

Sideboard. *On it:* 2 silver candlesticks, tantalus, silver kettle with spirit lamp, champagne cooler, empty champagne bottle, 5 champagne glasses, silver tray with 5 tumblers, water jug, port decanter, soda syphon

Desk. *On it:* Ashtray, table lamp, pentray, blotter, cigars

6 dining-room chairs

Armchair

Coal scuttle

Fire-irons

On mantelpiece: Marble clock, 2 bronze figures

On wall below fireplace: Telephone directory

Personal: **Gerald:** Ring in case, cigarettes in case
Birling: Cigar cutter
Inspector: Photograph

ACT II

On stage: No change

Personal: **Sheila:** ring

ACT III

On stage: No change

Personal: **Gerald:** ring

LIGHTING PLOT

Property fittings required: 3 wall brackets (*the one stage* L. *to be controlled separately*), 4 branched candlesticks with pink shades, 1 table lamp with pink shade, on desk

To open: All fittings ON: except wall bracket, stage L.
No. 1 batten: 1 circuit 54 pale rose, 1 circuit 3 straw
Floats: 1 circuit open white
Amber strip outside door
Spots to cover: fireplace and armchair (54 *pale rose*), downstage R. of table (3 *straw*), downstage L. of table (3 *straw*), upstage R. of table (54 *pale rose*), upstage L. of table (54 *Pale rose*), sideboard (54 *pale rose*)

Cue 1   **Birling** moves to the door and switches on the wall bracket
over the desk   (Page 7)
Switch on spot to cover desk down L. (54 *pale rose*)

No further cues. This lighting stands for the remainder of the play

EFFECTS PLOT

ACT I

Cue 1   **Birling:** ". . . mind his own business and look after
            himself and his own—and—"   (Page 7)
            Front door bell

ACT II

Cue 2   **Gerald:** "I don't think so. Excuse me." He goes out.
            Birling crosses upstage to the door to follow him, but
            as he reaches the door—   (Page 29)
            Front door slam

Cue 3   **Sheila:** "And can't you see, both of you, you're making
            it worse?"   (Page 30)
            Front door slam

Cue 4   **Sheila:** "Mother—I begged you to stop—" The **Inspector**
            holds up a hand   (Page 36)
            Front door slam

ACT III

Cue 5   **Inspector:** ". . . Good-night." He walks straight out   (Page 42)
            Front door slam

Cue 6   **Birling:** ". . . —and get to work quickly too."   (Page 44)
            Front door bell

Cue 7   **Birling:** ". . . And they can't even take a joke—"   (Page 52)
            Telephone bell

ALTERNATIVE
FURNITURE AND PROPERTY LIST

USING THREE SETS

ACT I

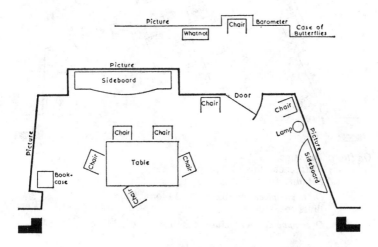

On stage: Dining table. *On it:* dish of fruit (centre-piece), 2 silver candlesticks, 5 dessert plates, knives and forks, 5 finger bowls, 5 port glasses, dish of nuts, nutcrackers, dish of sweets, glass match stand, white tablecloth

Sideboard, up R. *On it:* 2 silver candlesticks, cigar box, tantalus, silver kettle with spirit lamp, champagne cooler with empty bottle, silver tray with 5 tumblers, jug of water, port decanter, soda syphon, 2 used plates, 2 spoons, 2 forks

5 dining room chairs, Chippendale, 2 with arms

Tapestry chair, R. of door

Chinese Chippendale chair, L. of door

Sideboard, down L. *On it:* bronze figure, tray with 5 champagne glasses, 3 plates, 3 knives, 3 spoons

Standard lamp

Revolving bookcase. *On it:* Work-basket

In hall: Whatnot with brass pot and fern, chair, barometer, case of butterflies

On wall R.: landscape picture with cows

On wall over sideboard, up R.: landscape picture with cows
On wall L.: landscape picture—river scene
On wall in hall: picture of Trial Scene

ACT II

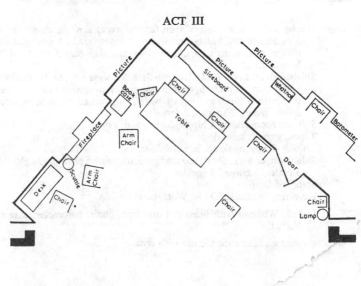

On stage: The same
    Add: fender, fire-irons, dogs
    2 leather armchairs

    On mantelpiece: marble clock, 2 bronze figures
    Brass coal-scuttle

    Over mantelpiece: picture of **Birling** as Lord Mayor

ACT III

On stage: The same
    Strike: sideboard, down L.

    Add: writing desk with bookcase above. *On it:* ashtray, telephone, table lamp, pen tray, blotter, telephone directory
    Chair at desk

    On return wall below desk: antelope horns

MADE AND PRINTED IN GREAT BRITAIN BY
LATIMER TREND & COMPANY LTD PLYMOUTH

MADE IN ENGLAND